SKIN

JEREMY POOLMAN

BLOOMSBURY

First published in Great Britain 2001
This paperback edition published in 2002

Copyright © Jeremy Poolman 2001

The moral right of the author has been asserted

Bloomsbury Publishing Plc, 38 Soho Square, London WID 3HB

A CIP catalogue record is
available from the British Library

ISBN 0 7475 5308 4

10 9 8 7 6 5 4 3 2 1

Typeset by Hewer Text Ltd, Edinburgh
Printed in Great Britain by Clays Ltd, St Ives Plc

SKIN

Interesting Facts About the State of Arizona

Audacity's Song

My Kind of America

A Wounded Thing Must Hide:

In Search of Libbie Custer

For Jan, Joasia, Hugh and Ewa

It is forbidden to forget, it is forbidden to be silent.

Primo Levi,
L'Echo dell'educazione ebraica

Here goes nothing

SELDOM, it seems, is a man asked to account for his life in anything but the most extreme circumstances. Well, such circumstances exist for me now. Mr Sikorski (my lawyer) tells me that once the authorities have sorted out their bungling attempts at 'firing up' our rather antiquated system of justice and the expected trial begins I will have little time for cool reflection, and that I should therefore seize the first opportunity that presents itself before then to set down on paper what he insists on referring to as my 'terrible story' – presumably in the hope that such a story will provoke the appearance of tears in the eyes of my peers, and that those tears will turn to pity and that pity, then, to acquittal. Not that he's said as much, you understand. I do, however, believe this to be the plan.

Some plan.

Some lawyer, Mr Sikorski.

Ah well.

With little to lose and what remains of a life to gain, I

suppose I might as well follow the young fool's advice – especially now that Ewa, in leaving when she did (oh it seems like only this morning), has presented me with this chance.

So.

Here, as Lennie would say, *goes nothing*.

How, though, to begin?

At the beginning, you say. Very well. I shall begin, then, with my days as a boy – my days as a boy with a father. In those days, after all, I was still (as they say) a blank canvas, still a clean pair of hands – still as yet (or so I believed – wrongly, as it turned out) an empty page unmarked by pen or brush, and as yet still unshat upon by all those flaming turds that would later shower down on me from the sky.

Anyway.

I should make a start.

First, though, before I do, a deep breath, for, to misquote (I think) Flaubert, a man must be calm before telling the wildest of tales.

So then, to begin

In my earlier days, whenever I came to believe I was nothing but a sinner and my life just a bad thing filled with unutterable hopelessness and despair, my father would remind me of what a wise man had once told him. He would climb the stairs to my eyrie here in the attic (I would hear him approaching, feel the weight of his shoes on the rickety steps), then he'd slowly lift the hatch — pushing with all his strength — so flooding the darkness with light. 'Janek,' he would say, 'are you there?' 'Yes, Papa,' I'd reply, aware once again, with the tremulous breaking of my voice, of the unmanly shame of my tears. 'I'm sorry, Papa,' I'd say, but he'd just smile and tell me *ssh*. Then he'd pick his crippled way slowly around these boxes filled with junk, bending low to avoid the beams, and ease down here below the window overlooking Florianska Street, and here he'd sit beside me for the longest of times, saying nothing — sitting hunched-over and quiet for so long sometimes, with his eyes closed tight as if he were trying to recall something from so long ago, that I'd start to think maybe he'd fallen asleep. But then in time he'd open his eyes as if he'd worked something out at last, and he'd lay his hand on my shoulder the way Father Rybicki used to do and tell me again what that wise man had said.

Which was?

Well it shames me now to tell you I don't know. Oh believe me, I have tried so many times to retrieve those words – closing my eyes so tight sometimes that sometimes they really hurt – tried to bring them back so that I might pass them on, but always there's nothing. Just silence. I used to think if only I tried hard enough that I'd hear them again – those strange-sounding words – and everything that was going wrong would somehow start going right – but I don't believe it any more. I believe they are gone now for ever – those words – as surely as is my father and his father before him. I believe now I will never get them back, however hard I try – and even then, if I did, what good would it do? They were – and would be still – lost in a language that I cannot – never could – understand. It was the language of the dying, of the betrayed and forgotten. It would be as ancient to me now as the language of the camps, as distant now as the words of Jesus Christ himself on the cross . . .

And yet, and yet . . .

And yet it seems to me sometimes that even that which the mind forgets leaves a kind of shadow, and I believe it is that shadow now – now with the year and even the century turning – that sits on my shoulders tonight, wrapping itself around me, bundling me up against this sharp December cold and warming me now with the fierce young heat of the past.

The snows of December

THIS morning I received no fewer than twenty-seven e-mails – all but one from my students: their number, I must shamefully reveal, the result of several weeks' inattention. There *was* a time (before all this nonsense blew up) when – holidays or not (not that you could really call these past weeks a holiday, considering) – I'd have checked them every day, responding then to each with the speed and care befitting a professor of American literature here at the grand old University of Krakow. Of course, not being twenty-five any more no doubt has something to do with it too (not to mention my current inability to sleep through the night without dreaming hard and bitter dreams) – just as, no doubt, it has a great deal to do with my recent obsession with exercise. In fact, it is this obsession for which I can thank my present situation – namely the damage done, four days ago now, to my right knee (this the result of cycling *too hard too quickly without first warming up*, as I was unsmilingly informed by Sonia, my 35-year-old leotard-wearing hard-bodied instructor – and all, for God's sake, on a machine going absolutely nowhere) – a moment of foolishness for which, in turn, I can thank my new (if temporary) life of leisure.

Not, you understand, that it's all just sitting around.

Oh no. On the contrary.

Only this morning, indeed, conscience at last persuaded me (*me*, for heaven's sake, an at least temporarily one-legged cripple, heroically exhausted by discomfort and dreams) to at last try and fix Ewa's friend Wojciech's crappy Russian bicycle – the result of which (my having agreed to this folly in a moment of quite absurd fatherly pride) being this: me, the professor, sitting on my aching backside in this stinking gloomy attic when I *should* be preparing my Fitzgerald seminar. Ah well. Such, I suppose, is how way leads on to way – not that, I'm sure, Frost had an attic-room in Poland in mind, but all the same. You just never can tell where any day's going to lead you is the point. I mean, you wake up one morning and there's chaos all around you, children screaming and everything going off like fireworks; you wake up the next day, there's silence. *Or*, of course, you find yourself struggling like an old man up some ladder that any minute is bound to collapse (and the climbing of which, I can tell you now, has made my knee even worse than before) in pursuit of a tool-box you haven't laid eyes on for fifteen years, and haven't even thought about for ten. And all to try and fix a bicycle belonging (or so he *claims*) to your daughter's best friend's former boyfriend – an unwashed snorting creep whose year of national service evidently equipped him with nothing more useful to the rest of us than a working (and I believe much-practised) knowledge of house-breaking. All of which right now seems like a sacrifice well

6

above and beyond the call of duty. Ah but then, I suppose, what is a father for if not to sacrifice his life for his child?

But enough, enough. As my own father would say, *Don't forget, Janek, there's always the Foreign Legion.*

So Polish, my father.

Such a memory, me.

You know, it occurs to me that I probably haven't thought about those words for nearly twenty years – probably not since the day, in fact, I last spent any time by this window. *Then*, of course, I was twenty years younger, and the streets of the city were not as they are today. *Then* there was silence and waiting. *Then* there was nothing but static on the radio. *Then* there was just the thunderous beating of my heart and the sound of Fredzio's screaming in my head.

Fredzio.

Fredzio.

Oh how strange to be thinking of him now – now, after all these silent years.

How strange and haphazard is this process of remembering.

Remember, remember the snows of December.

And how affecting it is now to think of such a brother at such a time – now, when I can scarcely ever have been less in need of a family, and more in need of the kindness and understanding of strangers.

Which reminds me

IVE a photograph of Tennessee Williams on the wall of my office which I keep there to cheer myself up whenever I feel down. In the picture, the great man is standing beside a swimming pool (Hemingway's, I think), his hands thrust deep in his pockets, his face quite contorted with laughter. Although it used to make me smile, these days it just serves to make me shake my head, representing as it does for me now my own duplicity. You see, at the height of what I can now dignify (now, with the soothing passage of time) by calling our 'affair' (a description, I regret to say, shared neither by the police nor those members of the faculty disciplinary board concerned with my case), I promised it to my daughter Ewa – knowing full well of course that I had already promised it to Rachel. That, in the end, neither was to get it is perhaps (in the face of such generosity on my part) somewhat ironic – particularly so since the Great American Playwright, so famous for his torturing of women on the stage, is still hanging on the wall above my desk (having outlasted them both), still smiling, his hands still thrust deep in his pockets, the laces of his tennis-shoes still so casually but so neatly tied.

But I digress

As I was saying.

Fredzio.

You know, I still remember as if it were yesterday the first time I saw him. He was beating his head against the schoolyard wall. He was ten years old and so was I. And I remember, too, the *last* time I saw him ten years later – nearly twenty years ago now – when he was back in that same schoolyard, the wound that, as a schoolboy, he'd been so anxious to create (the blood from which he'd hoped would be enough to give Mr Czerski, our history teacher, a heart attack – and enough, therefore, to postpone, perhaps indefinitely, the return of our essays entitled *Why the Individual is Nothing and the Party is Everything*) now streaming blood, and his corpse so riddled with what I knew to be bullets that, had his face not been left eerily unmarked (in death he was smiling, I recall, as if Mr Czerski had at last fallen and the essays been abandoned after all these years), there would have been scarcely enough to determine whether in life the body had been that of some slight boyish man or some tall gangling girl who'd strayed once too often from the straight and narrow path and had paid a gruesome price. As it was, even with his face plain for all to see, not a soul stepped forward to identify him. Not even I, his friend. Back then, in those first days of martial law, only a fool would raise his hand. In those days the milicja were everywhere.

I remember that evening, December thirteenth, nineteen eighty-one – the details of it – as sharply as tonight – that very day's nineteenth anniversary – I can pick out from up here the figures down below in Florianska Street as they head home, huddled up against the cold. From up here I can even see Borowski across the street in his room. He's watching football on his old black-and-white TV, Poland against (I think) Sweden, the shifting blue light throwing shadows around the walls, his great belly straining like a basketball in his vest. Oh I remember how he just cried that first night (he'd been so full of plans, so fired-up, so *alive* with the trouble he would make), and how the world had seemed suddenly like a world thrown into reverse, its gears raging, sheering, grinding like the heavy grinding tracks on the cobblestones below. And I remember my mother, breathless, tears rolling down her face, holding on to me so tight while at the same time begging me to go – but go where? *America*, she kept saying, *America*, although she knew as well as I it was too late for that.

The door was closing – had closed.

'I can't,' I said. 'No one can.' But I could tell she wasn't listening. I could tell she was thinking of my father. 'I'll go and find him,' I said. 'Bring him back.' She was thinking, I knew, of his fine craftsman's hands – how they had saved him once, long ago, but would they do so again? He was old now, his fingers stiffened with the cruelty of age.

'No, it's too dangerous,' she said. She gripped my arm tighter. 'Stay here. He'll come when he hears the news.'

'But –'

'Ssh now,' she whispered. Her hand touched my brow.

'Tomorrow then,' I said. 'I'll go tomorrow.'

'Yes,' she said. 'Tomorrow.'

Speaking of my father

'First the Nazis,' he used to say, 'now the Communists. What next, the *Jews*?' I never understood what he meant: everyone knew the Jews were all gone. Everyone knew (thanks to no higher an authority than Mr Czerski himself) that what was left of the Jews had fled west after the war before the righteous reclamation of the glorious Red Army, unable to contemplate life under socialism with its fairness, equality and care for the weak. Everyone knew this, it seemed, but my father. What, I used to wonder, was wrong with him? Why did he persist with such foolishness? *Just wait,'* he used to say, as if later that very day all those who'd been forced to flee would return in columns bent on revenge against those who'd betrayed them – those friends and neighbours whose whispers and shrouded fingers had condemned them to the cattle-trucks and the gas chambers and the pits filled with lime. It was as if only he could see something that the rest of us were blind to – as if he knew a secret that he never planned to share.

Of course, as it turned out, he *did* know a secret – the most fearful – the most *personal* – of secrets – but one I would only discover years after his death, and then quite by chance.

I still, though – despite everything – leave flowers at the grave he shares with my mother. In death, it is only for God to separate the good from the bad – for none of us is without sin, and none of us could withstand the cruel judgement of man.

But again I digress

Again, as I was saying.

Fredzio.

Right from the start – from the moment I saw him hitting his head on that wall in the schoolyard – saw his grin and the blood streaming vivid down his face and into the corner of his mouth – I knew he and I should be friends. He was obviously special – reckless and brave – everything, in fact, that I was not (I was a coward and went weak at even the *sound* of the word blood) – everything, indeed, that a friend should be. With his unkempt hair and scuffed-up shoes, he was quite the wildest character I had ever seen.

'So do you want to go canoeing?'

He was the person – the hero – I was in my dreams made flesh.

'Canoeing?'

We were standing at the tram-stop one afternoon after school. It was late April – maybe a month after the schoolyard incident – and the first time he ever addressed me. He scowled. 'Yes, *canoeing*,' he said, his tone that of one who is stuck on a tram with an idiot and must make do. He shook his head, dismissing. 'You do *go* canoeing, don't you?'

'Of course,' I said. 'All the time.'

'So you'll come then?'

I could feel myself blushing at the half-lie. It was true, I did often go along with my father and his friend – down to the mountains in my father's friend's old Skoda – but my father always said I was too young to paddle, my chest too narrow still for a life-jacket. So I always stayed on the bank, watching over the bags, sitting in the car if it rained.

'So?'

'So what?' I said, stalling. The thought of actually (maybe) going on the water was both thrilling and terrifying.

Fredzio Szczurek sighed. '*So do you want to?*'

I shrugged, attempting a casual air. 'I don't mind,' I said. 'When?' I tried not to think of my father – of the beating *for my own good* I'd get if he ever found out.

'Friday,' said Fredzio.

I couldn't stop a gasp. '*Friday?* But that's a *school* day!'

'So?'

'But –'

What occurred to me then was so shocking that it blew all the breath from my body. He couldn't be serious.

'*But it's . . . it's May Day!*'

Another shrug, this time in concert with a grin.

He was serious all right. I couldn't believe it. No one ever went canoeing on May Day – no one even dared ever fall ill. Everyone was always either in the main square, watching the procession – each of us waving our little red and red-and-white flags – or at home watching the Moscow Parade on TV.

'But I can't,' I said.

'It's up to you,' said Fredzio. Already he was turning away. I had to think fast.

'But what if somebody sees us?'

He paused, turned back.

'Are you scared?' he said.

I shook my head. 'No,' I said, 'of course not' – not adding, then, that I wasn't so much scared as terrified.

May Day was three days away – three days that, for me, were days of torment. The lessons in Citizen Training were the worst. There was I, listening intently to Miss Kozal as she told us (as she did every year, though each year with less animation – a diminution due, it was generally held, to old age and the consequent onset of all manner of ghastly ailments) of glorious sacrifice, and the need for each one of us to consider ourselves nothing more than a cog in our great and glorious socialist machine, while all the time there I was, a desperate subversive, a lover of self and shallow amusements. Every moment, at every turn, I expected the great hand of Comrade Gierek to descend – to clap me on the shoulder, so revealing my shameful secret to all and setting in train, then, my banishment from my family and all that I knew. In fact, so certain was I that all would be revealed (surely my guilt would in time creep its way from my bones until it was as obvious on my face as a suntan) that I would lie awake at night rehearsing my statement of regret over and over again – how I had been weak and led astray, but had come to my senses at last, and knew, now, my duty. But somehow – miracle of miracles – morning always came without my being found out, until *that* morning – Friday – was upon me.

I lay in my bed, at a little after seven, my heart thumping, listening to my mother climb the stairs. She tapped lightly on the door. 'Janek?' she said. 'Are you awake?'

'Yes, Mama.' Oh how, I wondered, would she cope with all the flashbulbs and questions? And wouldn't Papa lose his job at the tannery?

'Don't go back to sleep now.'

I said no, I wouldn't. I listened to her steps growing fainter. I felt so utterly miserable that I wished I was dead.

At breakfast, not a word was spoken (Mama and Papa had had some kind of an argument – over me I was certain) – and when Papa left for work (what he did was so important he didn't get released to go and see the procession) he slammed the door so hard that Mama's glass ornament from Vienna with snow that started falling when you shook it fell off the mantelpiece and shattered. A bad omen, if ever there was one. As usual, I kissed Mama's cheek at the door. I was certain it would be the last time I ever saw her.

The plan was not to be seen talking to one another at school (you could never tell who was listening), or to even stand together, and to meet again only on the Friday morning on the corner of Mikolajska Street and Krzyza. Until then, we didn't know each other, and weren't to acknowledge each other, even with a look. *Don't be late* had been Fredzio's last instruction, followed by something I didn't catch about a surprise.

Well, seven fifteen came and went, and no sign. I was just getting ready to turn gratefully away (there was still time, I hoped, to get to school and have my lateness go unnoticed), when a big old Russian car pulled up, the blast of its horn making me jump. Of course my only thought then was *they've got me* — that it was all some kind of set-up, a test of my loyalty — but though I told my legs to run, they would not. Even they had turned against me, stranding me there to await my ghastly fate.

Another toot of the horn. All around me, people were staring, suspicious of such a show. I gazed around at them, trying for a look of nonchalance, but they weren't concerned with me: they were looking at the car — the men, despite themselves, admiringly. Some, despite their fear, were even bent over, trying to peer in through the blackened-out windows. Suddenly the kerb-side window cranked down.

'Hey, you coming or what?' The voice was a voice I knew.

I dipped down. '*Fredzio?*'

'Quick. Get in.'

The window cranked up.

For a second I was speechless. A car! And Fredzio was driving it! It was too fantastic to be true.

Another toot of the horn, a revving of the huge, clanking engine, a great plume of dirty smoke. My legs, quite of their own accord, started moving. I watched my hand reach out, my fingers wrap themselves around the once-bright but now corroded handle. I pulled. The door opened, the air inside hitting me in that moment with the smoke from a huge thick cigar.

I looked hard at Fredzio — scarcely believing my eyes — but Fredzio, his teeth clenched like some gangster on the end of the cigar, and his backside set firmly on his schoolbag, had his hands gripping tight to the huge ancient wheel, and was peering out across the dashboard, looking for all the world like some remote and mysterious leader come to spy in disguise on an ungrateful people.

The rest of that day went by in a blur: the bouncing on thick springs along uneven roads, our laughter at the peasants who couldn't believe their eyes, the thick manly stench of cigar-smoke and the tortuous grinding of gears, the first sight of the mountains rising blue and magnificent and the hissing and gurgling of the fast-running river. All so long ago now, it seems, still, like a dream – just as it did at the time. At the time, it was as if I'd broken unexpectedly through some invisible wall – been released from the grey to the endless rolling green – and all thanks to Fredzio. To me, on that day, Fredzio Szczurek showed me quite what was possible. Of course I didn't know then, as we spun across the rapids and, later, as we dozed, exhausted, in the shade of a tree, that such release is never permanent except to the mad, and that only the mad need never return.

On the subject of which

MY father.

Yes, him again.

Ladies and gentlemen, it occurs to me now (although not *just* now, as this is something that's been with me, on and off, since childhood) that if, after all, man's notion of heaven turns out to be true, then He, like so many others, will most likely be up there looking down, watching me and listening to every word I say.

Not, of course, that I intend to be intimidated by such a thought – by such a – what can I say? – *presence* overhead. Oh no. For it is my firm belief (this, something else carried over from my youth) that if heaven exists at all, then it is because we – each one of us – like conjurers create it, and so, consequently, have the equal and opposite power to dismiss it. In short, I believe, then, that I am only being watched if I *believe* I'm being watched – that I am only being judged if judgement is what I crave. Which I don't. Of course I don't. Why would anybody in their right mind invite such scrutiny? Would you?

But I wander.

Back, then, to my defence.

What I intended to mention here was my father and this wallet. My father, this wallet, and his role (or not) in its creation.

Which was?

Well here, ladies and gentlemen, lies the madness.

I ask you, where else but here in this wonderland would a tanner of my father's experience and expertise be generously employed in the largest tannery in Poland (perhaps in the whole of Europe, for all I know), only then to be told that – far from filling a position for which such experience and expertise made him suitable (and the persuasive nature of which had surely secured him a job in the first place) – that is, as a *tanner* – *his* role was to be that of Quality Controller (Number Two) – a position of such extraordinary and bizarre complexity that it had already (or so persistent rumour had it) left three hitherto strong men insensible and caused a fourth to jump fully clothed into the Vistula in December and, consequently, to break his neck on the ice in three places.

All of which is not to say that my father wasn't grateful for the work – for indeed he was. In those days, in the years just after the war, it was work or starve, so a man took whatever work he could find and asked no questions as to the sense of it.

But back to the job itself.

Back to this wallet.

By any standards, the work is shoddy in the extreme – the stitching already working loose (the fibres themselves are no stronger, surely, than human hair), and the leather so ineptly cured that, whenever you open the thing, the grotesque (of course) red dye, having leeched on to your fingers and the palms of your hands, sticks with such tenacity that it's really quite the Devil to remove.

Some, you might say, quality control.

Well yes.

Except, of course, that, in my father's case, poor stitching and casual dyeing of the reject-quality leather were two of the principal quality thresholds which, in his exalted position as Quality Controller (Number Two), he was charged with meeting – given that they were far cheaper to achieve (and therefore more appropriate for the merely domestic market) than those perhaps more international standards expected of his colleague, Mr Grachev, whose name-badge proclaimed him (as it had done for nearly twenty years) Quality Controller (Number One).

All of which sounds today, I know, quite crazy, and so deeply cynical and patronising that it seems it could scarcely be true. But it is. Ladies and gentlemen, you know it as I know it. You know as well as I the malice in that wonderland. Like me, and like my father, you need only consult the tips of your fingers and these blood-red palms for confirmation.

Yes, but that's not all

Oн no.

For there was other madness at work then too. There was the calculated and quite sane madness of blackmail — that means, so liberally applied, of quite wilfully and perversely turning bears into donkeys and heroes into spies, and then lamenting that corruption with fake tears of distress.

Oh yes.

There was this.

Of course there was this.

But there was more.

There was the gift, too, of division through fear of retribution — a skill honed on the empty, wind-devoured Steppes and in the cellars of Stalingrad — a talent, so delightful in its symmetry, for turning brother against brother and son against father — for creating and then nurturing those sacrificial circles without which the great engine of the state wouldn't run, and for which every one of us is responsible, every one of us guilty for the absence of our sabotage.

Every one of us, that is, but a few. For there *were* a few who broke free of the embrace – some even, then, turning back to face destruction.

But only a few.

Fredzio, for one.

And look, as they say, what happened to him.

But not only to him, of course.

Oh no.

Though the names of the others, now, escape me, their faces do not, and I see them, still, every night and every morning, watch them standing absent at the tram-stop, or sitting before me, bizarrely transformed, their eyes for ever clear now, watching me as I fumble, shakey-handed, with the water-jug and chipped glass on my desk, trying so hard to concentrate lest, in a moment of weakness, I let them gather too close – let them smother me as they themselves were smothered, and let them squeeze from my chest any life that remains – let them leave me for dead as Fredzio was left for dead – my corpse – like his – stiff and still in some alleyway, a feast for the darkness and the rats.

Fredzio, Fredzio.

Oh how distant now does even the most recent history sometimes seem – so distant as to seem without connection.

Fredzio. Dead. I hear it, but still can scarcely believe it.

The Rosary too.

We band of brothers.

Betrayed.

We happy breed.

And the cost of that betrayal still outstanding, the deed still unrevenged.

But not for ever, for the time is coming.

It is coming – for certain.

I can feel it.

But I'm jumping ahead

So.

To jump back.

Thus.

It was during a trip down to the Tatras Mountains in the summer of nineteen seventy-eight (by then I was eighteen, a student at the university, and had just bought my first – secondhand – canoe) that Papa's friend Karol heard the news that he was to be the next Pope. Although being the Archbishop of Krakow was grand, Pope was the big one – especially seeing as how no one (including himself) had given him more than an outside chance, what with him not being Italian, and there not having been a non-Italian Pope for about three hundred years. So, one minute the man paddling behind me was just an archbishop, then the telephone rings in the pocket of his life-jacket and he's Pope. Never having been so close to God's chosen representative on earth before, I didn't know what to do. I felt certain there had to be some sort of protocol to follow at times like this (I remember imagining a booklet entitled *What To Do If You're in a Two-Man Canoe and the Man Paddling Behind You Suddenly Becomes Pope*, and then feeling ashamed at such foolishness): I felt sure I should pull over to the bank at once – but then what? Prayer, maybe – or maybe just a few well-chosen words of congratulation? Anyway, I was just agonising over whether or not to lift my paddle from the water (in order to give some sort of salute), when a finger tapped me firmly on the shoulder, and a voice rose over the rushing of the water:

'*Stop, Janek! Stop!*'

I twisted in alarm, nearly tipping us over. '*What is it?*' I said. '*Are you all right?*'

But Karol – his face wet with spray – was turning and pointing frantically at the river behind him.

'What?' I shouted. '*What?*'

He turned back, shrugged a sheepish shrug. 'Too late now,' he said.

'Too late? Too late for what?'

He pointed again at the water spinning back and away. 'Your papa's telephone,' he said, shouting, cupping his hands to his mouth, 'I dropped it in the river.' He leaned forward, frowning hard. 'Oh I'm sorry, Janek,' he said. 'Do you think your father will ever forgive me?'

'Forgive you?' I said. 'But you're the *Pope*!'

For a moment, then, the face of Karol Wojtyla – usually so animated – went blank. It was then, I think, that the reality of his ascension really struck him.

It took me a while to get the canoe back to the bank (not only did I have to work against the current, but my companion seemed suddenly to have lost all interest in paddling), and by the time I had the thing tied up and we were sitting on a log waiting for my father to arrive with the car, the weather had turned – a blanket of grey clouds drawing slowly across the blue.

'So what are you thinking?' I said. He was staring out at the river, his hands thrust deep in the pockets of his jacket, his chin buried low beneath his collar.

'I was thinking about God,' he said.

'Oh?' I said, trying to sound casual.

He turned to me. His face was pale, his eyes troubled. 'Do you think,' he said, 'He really cares – about us, about Poland?'

'He must do,' I said. 'He chose you, didn't He?'

Embarrassed suddenly, I turned away. In a moment, I felt the touch of a hand on my shoulder. 'Bless you,' he said, as the first drops of rain began to fall.

We drove home in thoughtful silence (my father, I could tell, was driving now with much greater care than usual), along roads which, years ago, I'd travelled with Fredzio in his father's big old car. I couldn't help thinking, as we passed familiar landmarks, how fleeting is our time on this earth and how grand our plans, but how it is only the land that in the end endures.

By the time we got back to the city, the news was already out. Florianska Street was already packed with people, a jostling crowd, everyone waiting for the new Pope to arrive at the house of his friend. As we turned the corner, a little boy called out, 'There he is!', and every face turned. There was joy on each one, and such happiness – such pride – I'd not witnessed before, and scarcely imagine I will ever see again.

That night – all night – there was laughter and dancing. That night, suddenly, Poland had emerged from darkness into light. That night we knew we were as good as anybody. That night we had the Pope – so what now wasn't possible?

Oh, but wait now

Dont go away deceiving yourself (as I once did) that, following the great day (and it *was* a great day – don't ever forget it), everything started getting better straight away. You know and I know this is hardly the case. In fact, in many ways, things just started getting worse (you remember, surely, the spiralling prices? The simple impossibility of ever really getting enough to eat?), and, in some cases, are still doing so. And not just big things either – but small (you would think), insignificant things too.

Take football, for example.

Take tonight.

Now I would guess from Borowski's rather sudden change of demeanour (how he tossed his bottle against the wall before snapping off the TV and stomping from the room) that Sweden has beaten Poland in the Euro 2000 qualifiers, with the consequence (as I understand it, that being the case) that Poland won't be in Holland come the summer. Of course it would be far too Polish of me to draw any grim and altogether wider significance from this failure – it is, after all, only football.

However.

Lest I disappoint any non-Poles who might read these lines, let me just say this: unless you have lived through what we have lived through – the isolation, the grotesque and all-pervading incompetence, the straight-faced corruption – not to mention the huge and terrible (and scarce) Russian fridges (for which we were meant to be grateful) – then you cannot possibly understand how hurtful is our exile from something even as banal as a football tournament. Our absence will rekindle again our barely dampened feelings of hopelessness and self-disgust. *It's what we deserve*, people will start saying again, and we'll pull up the covers and again start to blame no one else but ourselves – when we should, of course, be blaming the Russians. And the Germans. And the Americans. And the English. In fact, everybody who's ever come this way (or *not*, in the case of the English) – but no. *It's all our own fault*, we'll all start saying. *It's what we deserve*.

Oh, you say (I see it in your eyes), for God's sake must you bring the war into everything? Can we never escape that wretched September day fifty years ago?

All right. I'll not mention it.

We just want to move on, you say.

I said all right.

We just want to forget.

To return then.

About time.

I was talking about the Pope and that day.

Those lies, you mean. We're not stupid.

OK, OK, all right? – so I lied. Big deal. I lied about being there on the water with him when Papa's friend was made Pope. And, yes, I lied about the mobile phone. By then I hadn't even *seen* such a thing (and wouldn't do for another fifteen years) – but what the hell? I mean, it's not as if I didn't *go* canoeing with him before *and* after his elevation – because I did – and, besides, what's wrong – what's so inaccurate – about a little reorganisation? Just call it, if you like, the poetic licence of the incarcerated man. Or, for that matter, anything else you choose. But whatever you call it, just let me get on – all right? You may have all the time in the world; I, however, do not.

So.

Now.

I was talking about how (foolishly, it seems now, and so so naive), following that great day, we really thought we'd wake up the next and everything would have changed – all doors that had hitherto been double-locked and bolted flung open, and skies that had seemed for so long nothing but grey, blue now, and the overnight streets decked out come morning with streamers as if it was Christmas come early and for ever, and banners proclaiming our righteous liberation.

But we know all this.

All nonsense, of course.

Don't forget we were there too.

Although it *was* to come. In time, of course, the great bear would stumble and, indeed, within just three years, would crash, helpless, to the ground – though not so helpless that it couldn't keep a twitch going out of sight of the revellers – couldn't keep a single finger on a solitary hand curling and uncurling with life, as we, the victors, prodded the carcass – timid at first, but then reckless as drunks – all believing, like our fathers before us and their fathers before them, that the war – for so long undeclared – was finally and irrevocably over.

We *said* don't mention the war

ALL right, all right. I'm sorry.

Sorry isn't good enough. Look, isn't there anything to drink?

What?

I said sorry isn't good enough.

Well it's all I've got.

You've got no idea, have you?

I *said* I'm sorry.

No cushions. No drinks. Jesus.

Jesus Christ. Have you finished? Can I get on now?

For heaven's sake, just how long are we to be here without anything to drink?

Oh great. My life's in the balance and all the jury wants is something to drink.

And cushions. Don't forget cushions.

Screw you.

That's not wise, young man.

Yeah, whatever. I'm moving on. Now, as a young man, my

father's great hero was General Custer, and he'd spend hour after hour poring over the maps and photographs his friend Lennie would send him from America, fighting and re-fighting Appomatox and the Washita and, of course, the Little Big Horn –

You should show us some respect.

Jesus. What *now?*

Nothing. Go on.

Right.

We're just saying you should think before you speak –

I said right – OK?

OK.

Right. Well. He *used* to say it was through trying to decipher the books Lennie sent him that he learned to speak English as well as he did – which fact, of course, would also explain how, until the day he died, he barely uttered a sentence in English that didn't sound like the description of some military campaign. To him, a trip out to the shops was always 'going out scouting', whilst, apparently, often when they did go out, he'd insist (much to her understandable annoyance) on referring to my mother as 'Miss Libbie' – in honour, of course, of the general's widow. In fact, so obsessed did he become that I'm told that when I was born he'd wanted to call me George, but my mother put her foot down, insisting I be called Janek after her father and his father before him.

Is that it?

No. There's more. For God's sake give me a chance. There was another, far more serious consequence of my father's youthful obsession. It was what, in the end, would rob him prematurely of that very youth – by leading him, like a lamb is led, to the scene of great slaughter and defeat on the field of battle, and then down into the darkness of Auschwitz and his labour in the Monowitz-Buna rubberworks.

How so?

Well, the cavalry, of course. Following in the footsteps of his idol, my father joined the cavalry.

OK, so tell us about that then.

OK. Well, historians record that, in nineteen thirty-eight, Poland had perhaps the greatest army in Europe – in the Europe, that is, of *eighteen* thirty-eight. Barely any planes, and no tanks to speak of, she trusted her safety to the squadrons of cavalry who'd not known defeat since the Swedish invasion of Charles XII. Their victory, it was thought, in the coming war with Germany was certain, and there was even talk of marching on Berlin (with the cavalry, of course, taking the vanguard) and hanging the Führer from the middle of the Brandenburg Gate. The war, everyone believed, would be short and glorious. Poland would gain a victory that, once and for all, would mean peace and security, her future assured. The only problem with all this was that nobody told the Germans – and although the war, when it came, was certainly short – two weeks at most – for Poland and her cavalry (whose flesh and horsehair were no match for the steel of Panzer tanks), the only glory to be had was whatever glory can be found in a swift and glorious death.

And your father? Where did he say he was in all this?

My father surrendered, after six days of fighting, at Wester-platte on the outskirts of Danzig, having had (like his hero Custer before him) his horse shot from under him. He and Lennie and three others were held for three days in a barn with neither food nor water, after which they were herded at gunpoint into one of fifteen or so cattle-wagons – each one of which was already packed so tight with prisoners from the Front that only the tallest (my father amongst them) could find any room to breathe. Many died on the journey, and after arriving three days and three nights later at the train's destination, their bodies were removed by inmates of the camp and carried straightaway to the crematoria. Also marched immediately to their deaths were the old, the sick and the very young – those for whom the Nazis had no use, except as sources to be plundered for gold (for barter), hair (for blankets), and body fat and skin that would be temporarily boiled to liquid or stretched over looms, the first useful in the production of soap, the second, souvenirs.

Souvenirs? What do you mean, souvenirs?

I *mean* souvenirs – OK? Anyway, as for my father and those others considered 'economically useful' to the Reich, their fate was to be worked until exhaustion or hunger or that slow, creeping atrophy of will overcame them, and they could struggle no more. From there it was but a short and silent journey to the gas chambers of Birkenau and thence to the furnace and the bitter freedom of the flames.

But your father survived. How?

Yes, and, thinking about it now, I can scarcely believe how little I knew about that part of his life while he was alive (that is, how little he told me, for the strength of his silence I like to think made my asking impossible), and it amazes me now to think that it took his very death (and then Rachel's shaming incredulity at my ignorance) to make me realise the importance of a man's private history – make me realise how impossible it is to ever really understand and have compassion for the worst of a man's sins – even if they be wilful, even if they be unforgivable in their consequences – without understanding the depth of the night within which those sins were conceived.

You still haven't said how he survived.

He survived is all. A blessing.

A what?

And a curse. A blessing and a curse.

This morning

YET another box of books from New York. This is the third delivery in as many weeks – a situation that I can't help feeling is getting out of hand. For heaven's sake, Lennie must be nearly eighty now, and what with his suffering from Parkinson's disease (to the extent that his handwriting that always was hard to read – typical doctor – is now just about unintelligible), I really rather wish he'd stop, as, increasingly these days, each book I receive carries with it a cost in guilt (the thought of him dragging himself around the bookshops of the city, getting up and down stairs and on and off the subway, makes me cringe) that, to be honest, I'm becoming less and less willing to pay.

But anyway.

Amongst today's offerings (mostly new novels by – to me – unknown Americans of a liberal leaning) is something called *A Wounded Thing Must Hide – In Search of Libbie Custer*, a book written by someone called Russell Gilchrist. How it found its way in amongst the fiction I don't know. I suppose he thought my father would have liked it, and that maybe I'd like it too. I don't know but it seems like an odd kind of book – a sort of dual biography of both subject and author – one in pursuit of the other across continents and a century – and whether this works (I'll admit that the idea intrigues me) we shall for the time being just have to wait and see. What with so much still to do on my seminar, I really have little time for much reading these days. Which, it occurs to me now, is perhaps a little ironic, given that I am, for the time being at least, to all intents and purposes, thanks to my knee, a solitary prisoner here in this attic, with, consequently, little but time on my hands.

On the subject of which.

It seems I have been joined by (probably) a mouse (I don't like to think it's a rat) that I've decided to call Stanislaw – Staszek for short. Although I haven't actually *seen* him yet (they say you never see the one that gets you), I know he's here because I've heard him. He's been gnawing away behind the boxes in that far corner. I suppose he must be wary of me at the moment, although as soon as he realises that, with *my* knee, I am, for the time being at least, immobile and therefore no threat, that, I imagine, will change. Who knows, maybe then he'll come out of hiding and say hello.

Oh but listen to me going on. What would Ewa and her friends think if they could hear me now? Not to mention her mother. Rachel always *did* say I was too solitary for my own good, and that she wouldn't be at all surprised if one day I started talking to ghosts and shadows.

Well, it seems that day has arrived. Or maybe it arrived long ago and I just didn't notice. Maybe I've been talking and talking for years without really being heard. If this is the case, I can't say it would particularly surprise me. In fact, I've often had the feeling lately, when I'm standing up in front of all those students – all those fresh young eyes and clear-beating hearts – when I'm saying my piece about Edith Wharton or Henry James or the myth of the greatness of *The Catcher in the Rye* – that it's only me now that's really listening, and that those eyes and those hearts are longing to be free of me – free to pursue that which is really important – that which really *counts* – which is life, of course, not art. But then sometimes I think, does it matter? Surely we're all alone anyway in a darkness of our own making, and the only voices we really hear (apart from those voices in our heads, which, anyway, are only ever our own voices so synthesised through the veil of our memories and dreams that they become in the end unrecognisable) are those we hear muffled by the width of a wall – voices whose words we wilfully mangle and misinterpret until they prove to us once again the indisputable presence of all we long for and fear . . .

But *then* . . .

Then I start thinking maybe art really is the only way out of this nightmare – that maybe only through art can those lies and misinterpretations be made to make up any kind of pattern, and so be persuaded to provide that neatness and order we all in our hearts crave.

But I suppose, in the end, the truth is I don't know. I *used* to know – I used to be certain. Just as I used to be sure that I'd be here tomorrow, and that this belly I have been slowly acquiring would never appear, and that I'd never be as old as my father was when he and my mother had me. But you look away once, look back, and it's here – the unbelievable future – having crept up in plain sight to stand before you as broad-winged and sharp-beaked as some giant mirthless bird.

Like a raven maybe

OR one of those scavenger birds that circles overhead as our hero, cast adrift in the desert, trips and stumbles on some sharp, gnarly stump, only to lie there then, exhausted, ready at last – indeed, grateful – for the peace to be found in death's final release.

Or maybe (it occurs to me now) a canary.

Like Burt Lancaster.

(Bear with me.)

In that movie? *The Birdman of Alcatraz*?

Or (of course) like Lennie himself.

Who (and this has always seemed strange to me, and seems strange to me still) has never (at least in his letters), even despite his admittedly brief and not really so unpleasant period of dubiously constitutional imprisonment, expressed any bitterness towards America – indeed, quite the contrary. In fact, it always seemed to me, from what others said (principally, of course, my father, who must, in this, as in all things, of course be believed), almost as if his having been shipped out to that island simply confirmed in his mind the rightness of his choice – that, for such a dedicated, unreconstructed latter-day Marxist, really the only place to be was in a six-by-four cell in a capitalist prison on an entirely featureless rock in the middle of the bay of San Francisco. It was as if such nominally harsh and unreasonable treatment of an entirely legal refugee (albeit such a troublesome one), following on as it had from the equally gratuitous hounding he'd received from those fakers in Moscow from whom he'd so fortuitously escaped, served merely to underline the purity of his vision – so obviously unpalatable as it was to both former friend and present foe alike.

Which is not to say he wasn't glad of his release when it came – although this, of course, he denies still, and will no doubt go to his pre-paid sunny-side-of-the-hill Westchester County grave still denying, professing, as he doubtless will be, his enduring regret at this most untimely and inappropriate removal.

All of which is not to say that he ever lost the fervour of his what was obvious to everyone entirely fake convictions – just that those convictions were allowed to find, in the land of the free, circumstances more conducive to their elegant expression; and besides (as he took to advising my father), what use is there preaching to those who already know the lesson?

What indeed.

The crippled old charlatan.

Getting out when he did and not telling my father.

Getting out when he did and leaving my father to struggle and suffer from within.

Not, of course, to be fair (and we must always be fair), that my father had the range of Lennie's choices. He was useful all right – an example to others – but, in the end, no scientist. Indeed, due to his choice that was no choice all those years ago, his choice now was a choice of one. He had no exit and no chance of one. And anyway, who flees the house when it's friends come to call?

Well?

Well what?

Oh, so you *are* awake.

No. We're asleep. But carry on anyway. You're not really telling us anything.

I am. I'm saying about my father.

OK.

What does that mean?

It means get on with it. We haven't got all day.

Yes you have. You've got as long as it takes to find me guilty.

That's for us to decide. Now, get on with it, will you?

You made me lose my place.

You said, 'Who flees the house when it's friends come to call?' Whatever that means.

Oh yes.

Right.

Who indeed?

Whatever.

And *especially* when those friends know you've nowhere else to go – no other friends – and when they know what you did – which rivers have been crossed – and so know the lie of the country ahead.

The lie of the country,
the depth of the river

I REMEMBER hearing tell of the bodies of criminals that could be found every morning washed up on the Vistula's banks – and how (so Fredzio would tell me, his face lighting up, as if what he was saying was quite the most amusing thing that ever could be heard) – how, every morning, at first light, the soldiers would come in their diesel-spewing trucks, ready to gather up the night's gruesome bounty. *I've seen them*, he'd say, and he'd describe in great detail how, with ungloved hands quite blue from the cold, they'd teeter, then, the soldiers, like old ladies down the slippery banks, their voices hanging sharp in the heavy morning mists, and how, then – two to a corpse – they'd heave and curse their way back up the bank and then – quite careless, as if their burdens were nothing but bags of cement or potatoes – toss the bodies into the backs of their trucks. Then the trucks would fire up and, all blue smoke and grinding gears, make their way back whence they had come. The whole process would take, apparently, no more than ten minutes –

and was, I believed, a complete and utter fabrication. *No, it's true*, he'd say, quite wounded (this, when enough time had passed for me to feel secure enough in our friendship to make such an observation), and he'd try to persuade me to go with him next morning to see for myself.

It is only in looking back now – now with so much time having passed – that I know (or, perhaps, can admit to myself) quite why it was that I was so reluctant to go with him – how it was only when Krysztof said he'd go too that I agreed, and how it was, consequently, that I came to find myself, one morning at dawn in early September, standing still and quite unbreathing, looking down at the river from a copse of shadowed trees.

'Hey, Janek –'

I remember Fredzio's breath, the closeness of his cheek as we talked low in whispers, and how my eyes, despite the cold, were heavy still with sleep.

'What?'

'You ever heard of the Rosary?'

'The what?' And I remember, too, how Krysztof, who was some way off, had been shivering so badly I could hear his teeth chattering.

'The Rosary. The Living Rosary.'

I shrugged. The words rang some bell – but a bell so distant as to be scarcely audible.

'You must have –'

'I don't know. Maybe.'

'The fifteen decades of the rosary? One man for each decade? Oh come on, you must –'

Then, slowly, it came back to me. The fifteen young men and their devotion to Mary, Queen of Poland. I nodded, half shrugged. 'Yeah – so?'

'Well what do you think?'

'What do you mean, what do I think?'

Fredzio sighed. 'What do you *think* I mean?'

'I don't know.'

Another sigh. 'Look. Think about it. We're running about on our own, right –'

'*Hey* –'

'And getting nowhere –'

Across the way, half-lost in shadows of his own, Krysztof was pointing down towards the river.

'Look –'

On the road (the road was really nothing more than a track) that ran parallel to and a little above the river's far bank, there was an army truck now where a minute ago there'd been none.

I counted the soldiers disembarking – four, five, six. 'Jesus, where did they come from?'

'Sssh.'

Once out of the truck, they stood around just stamping their feet, some cupping their hands to their faces, some lighting cigarettes.

Fredzio turned to me. He was grinning. 'See?' he said. '*Now* do you believe me?'

'Maybe they broke down,' I said.

'They didn't break down.'

'Or maybe they're lost.'

Fredzio shook his head. 'Look.' Over on the far bank, one of the soldiers was pointing. I flicked my eyes down to the river.

'*Jesus.*'

There, at the river's edge, being lapped and caressed gently by the water, was what looked like a log caught in weeds. It was the colour of the river – grey and dirty brown – and the size, approximately, of a fully grown man. I felt my chest tighten and my throat suddenly go dry.

We watched in silence as two soldiers broke off from the group and edged gingerly down the bank. Boots sinking in the mud, they squelched their way over to the body. Here they stood a while, looking down at it, their manner seeming almost reverential – so much so, in fact, that, for a moment, I really expected them to drop to their knees in sorrowful prayer.

'That's fifty zlotys you owe me.'

But of course they didn't. On the command of the man by the truck, they just tossed away their cigarettes and stooped – one either end – then lifted the mound from the mud. Slowly, then, as if the weight were excessive, they made their way back up the bank – sometimes sliding a bit but always recovering – and then to the back of the truck. Then a few practice swings and the body was in.

Fingers nudged my ribs. I turned.

'Come on. Pay up.'

'What?'

Fredzio was still grinning. He curled his fingers back and forth. 'Pay up,' he said.

'What do you mean?'

'Are you saying you don't remember?'

'Remember what?'

'Our little bet, of course.'

'We didn't have a bet and you know it.'

Fredzio shrugged. 'Ah well,' he said. 'I guess you'll just have to be next.' He nodded towards the river. 'Didn't I mention that he who doesn't pay, pays?'

'Look,' I said.

'What?'

Across the river, the brittle sound of voices. The man by the truck was pointing again at the water.

Another dig in the ribs.

'Better make that a hundred,' whispered Fredzio.

We made our way home that day in silence, each one of us lost in our own separate thoughts. For me, I couldn't stop thinking about that first faceless bundle, and what it was he might have done — what crime he might have committed — that had brought about such an end. And later that night, lying in bed and listening to my father, to his cries reaching muffled through the wall, I tried to think of other things — tried to picture myself in some other, distant place — but, every time, could not — for, every time, the beaches I walked along turned in time into mud, and the hand of a lover every time into the ungloved pointing hand of a soldier.

So tell us about this Rosary

WHAT about it?
   Then it was real?
   Yes it was real.
   So then.
   What do you mean, so then?
   I mean tell us about it. Jesus Christ.
   There's nothing to tell.
   So it didn't exist.
   I *told* you it existed.
   You and that Fredzio — right?
   Me and Fredzio.
   And Krysztof.
   And Krysztof, yes.
   Anyone else?
   Yes.
   How many?
   I don't know. Borowski, for one.

You don't know?

OK – eleven, maybe twelve.

Twelve?

I just said that. Didn't I just say that?

OK, OK. We get the message. You don't want to talk about it.

I don't mind.

Is that because of what happened?

What do you mean?

Why you're reluctant to talk about it –

I'm not reluctant.

I mean, is it the fact that someone betrayed you?

No. I just don't see the point.

The point?

Of going over it all again.

Well that's rich – coming from you. All you do is ramble on.

Well *excuse me*, but did I ask to be here?

In a manner of speaking, yes.

That's crap.

No. It's the truth. It's obvious you're looking for something.

Like what?

Forgiveness maybe.

Forgiveness for what?

Or punishment. Whatever – that's what we're here for. To see that you get what you want. Oh, and by the way, do you have a message at all?

A message? What do you mean?

For your father.

My father?

No?

You mean he's here?

Of course he's here. He's always here. Like two peas in a pod, you two.

Jesus Christ.

I take it that means there's no message then.

What?

Then why not tell us about the Rosary instead? It was a kind of terrorist group — right?

No. We were rebels. Patriots. Not terrorists. They were the terrorists.

Yes of course.

And anyway, we hardly got to do anything —

Before you were betrayed.

Just paint a couple of slogans really.

By Borowski.

What?

You were betrayed by Borowski. Isn't that right?

Who said?

Nobody. It just seems to make sense. He is overweight after all. And he is here. Or rather, there.

Where?

Across the way. See him?

I can't see anybody.

Well he's there.

Are you saying it was him?

Either him or somebody else. Best make it him.

Why?

Because he's like that mountain.

What?

Just there. Available. Or like Jesus.

Jesus? What do you mean?

Ready to be sacrificed for our sins. Or, more accurately, yours.

I don't know what you're talking about.

Of course you don't. But you will. And, in the meantime, why don't you tell us about Las Vegas?

Las Vegas?

We'd like that. Will you tell us about Las Vegas? Oh go on!

Are you sure that's what you want?

Positive. Nothing would make us happier than to hear about the clocks in Las Vegas.

OK. If you're sure.

We're sure. Now, what should we call it – this story?

I don't know.

Well, I do. Let's call it

Viva Las Vegas

OK, OK – but there's something I want to say first.

There is?

About the Rosary. About Fredzio.

All right. Go ahead. If it makes you feel better.

Well it has to do with the watch.

The watch?

The one he stole and gave to me.

I didn't steal it.

Oh no – I forgot. He 'liberated' it. Tell me: how does that work? Does the corpse have to be cold before it's not stealing?

You don't understand how it was. He was desperate, and it was currency.

Yes I know. You said. Anyway, that's not the point.

So what is the point?

The point is I want you to know it found a good home.

What do you mean?

I mean I lent it – or rather gave it – to a friend.

You're going to tell me it was this Fredzio — right?

Right.

And he didn't have a watch of his own, I suppose.

Yes, but not the right kind.

All of which I'm supposed to understand.

His wasn't the kind with hands. His wasn't the kind you could take apart and reassemble.

I have no idea what you're saying.

The kind you'd want for a device.

You mean a bomb?

Precisely.

You mean he made a bomb?

I mean he made a bomb. Or rather, we did. All of us. We were all of us in it together.

Jesus Christ.

But don't worry.

What do you mean?

It didn't go off. It got intercepted. Anyway, that's what I wanted to say. I wanted to thank him.

What?

For the watch. And now, in a rather neat (although I have to admit unintentional) segue, back to Las Vegas and those clocks.

Hang on —

Now, what was it you suggested as a title?

You can't just leave it there —

Oh yes, I remember. It was

Viva Las Vegas

OK then. Here goes.

A friend from the faculty who has visited America told me once that there's not a single clock to be seen anywhere in any of the casinos in the city of Las Vegas. Apparently (so he said), day can pass into night and vice versa without a soul inside being aware of the fact. Of course, Jerzy being Jerzy, one should accept such an assertion only warily, it having also been stated by him as fact that when we all saw Jaruzelski shaking that day on TV it was because the Russians (for some crazy reason known only to themselves – and, of course, to Jerzy) had placed a bomb beneath his chair, and not because (as we all liked to think) the rumours of his recent incontinence were true.

Anyway, with regard to the question of the presence of clocks (or not) in Las Vegas, the more I think about it, the more inclined I am to believe that Jerzy was telling the truth. It seems to me now quite sensible for the owner of a casino to not want his customers to be aware of time's passing, for, were they to be so, then surely they would also be made aware of how swiftly the hours were moving (so many sunrises, so many sunsets), and, consequently, how profligate they were being with whatever time was left to them.

All of which, unnerving as it is (the idea, that is, of Jerzy telling the truth and not just his amusing 'entertainments'), has got me wondering just how many other things he's said over the years that I was wrong (we all were) to dismiss as simple tall stories. For example, could it really be true about Jaruzelski and that bomb (for heaven's sake it wouldn't be the first time our benevolent masters in the Kremlin have done such a fantastically stupid thing), and when we all laughed when he told us Fredzio Szczurek – our Fredzio – wasn't dead at all – that he'd just been faking – and that he had, in fact, been seen marching briskly in the Moscow Parade, proud in the uniform of a Red Army captain, were we perhaps all a little too quick to laugh a little too loud?

But then, on the other hand, one swallow (as they say) doesn't make a spring – and, besides, didn't I see Fredzio's body that day in Szeroka Square? Didn't I see his blood, so red on the stones? Or should I be starting to doubt now even the evidence of my own eyes? And, anyway, I'd have known – felt it surely – if it had been *him* that had betrayed us. Wouldn't I?

Oh but listen to me. In all probability there *are* clocks – dozens of them – in Caesar's Palace, and no doubt Jaruzelski still suffers from the shits. And Fredzio – mad, reckless Fredzio? Well, if I knew where his grave was, I would certainly take a trip there, lay some flowers on the stones. I would feel it – I know I would – if he were still alive. I would feel it like a man feels the presence of a brother.

There's someone here to see you

THERE is?

There is, yes.

Who is it?

He's right here.

Oh.

And he's been very patient.

Well he can wait some more. I've something to say first.

Just for a change.

Don't be sarcastic.

OK. Sorry. What is it?

Well, it occurred to me just now, thinking about it all again, just how gradual – how imperceptible in its advance – was his grasp on my life, and how foolish I was then to have ever thought myself his equal in anything that really counted – me, who was always so unwilling to really engage in anything the outcome of which I couldn't see, hear and touch: me – little Janek – to whom the very word change was enough to send running breathless and

scared, back into the safe, cloistered world of my parents' house –
of my room, of this attic from whose window all can be observed
without the watcher being seen –

*Look, excuse me butting in, but we thought you wanted to talk –
and he is waiting –*

Which, of course, is not to say that I didn't *want* that change
– that I didn't *want* those blue jeans and that ticket to Disney-
land. Oh no – on the contrary – sometimes I wanted them so
badly that I'd dream of them; some nights – all night – I'd be
riding those wild rollercoasters, the wind whipping my hair
back along with my screams, or gliding underwater, me and my
crew, dead quiet in Captain Nemo's submarine, only to wake
up next morning exhausted from all my night-time exertions
and unable entirely to believe that it had all been just a dream
and that there wasn't maybe just one little bit that hadn't maybe
been real –

*Was it about the river, maybe? Did you want to talk to your father
about the river?*

Which is all, in short, to say that though yes, of course, I
wanted change to happen (we all did), what I really wanted was
for that change *to have already happened* – for it to be already in
place, and for there to be no need, therefore, for any (of course
willing) contribution from me –

Hello?

(This, of course, lamentably – for had I not always held
myself in perpetual readiness?) Yes, the truth is that, like so
many others, what I really wanted – what I really knew I
deserved – was to wake up one morning to find everything
gone that was drab and dull, and for it all to have been replaced
by what was colourful and new –

Well did you?

I suppose what I'm saying is that I was in fact in my heart everything that Fredzio affected to despise (and so everything, by nodding my complicity in such disgust, I too found worthless and despicable) – what he, so dismissively and with such venom, would call 'tourists of the revolution' or 'whores of the Party' – those cowardly parasites who would no more raise their fists in defence of what is possible than they would in defence of their lives.

Well?

'*Come the day,*' he would whisper, and then I'd nod in agreement at the harsh and ghastly sentence he proposed would be passed upon such shallow hateful creatures, all the time wondering how it was that such a brilliant and clear-sighted fellow couldn't see what was right before his eyes – couldn't see that I was such a creature, and that – come the day – it would be I that would step back while he and the others stepped forward in order to man the barricades and so take their places in history amongst the nation's heroes.

Look, he's here. Right here. Waiting.

Why, I used to wonder, can he not see this?

Or rather he was. Now he's gone again. Jesus Christ, do you see what you've done?

Could it have been perhaps that he *did* see it – did see what I was (what I am still), but didn't *want* to see it, and so chose blindness for himself over the pain of disappointment? I just don't know. All I know is that he had some kind of faith in me – a faith I never had in myself – and for that I loved him and love him still. He was then – and is still – more than the brother I never had: he was – and is – me painted large in the colours of life – me, Janek Janowiec, son and father, drawn out of this darkness and into the new light of day.

Ten twenty-five

I THOUGHT I just saw Ewa crossing the road then entering the Mleczko Gallery with a friend – but it seems I was wrong. It was *her* going *in* all right (I could make out her mother's features quite clearly, despite having to lean so far out of this window that I swear I nearly fell), but by the time she came out it wasn't her at all. I suppose it must be my eyes. Maybe I should go and see Kozinski after all.

Ten thirty

THAT, by the way, and to avoid any further confusion, would be Kozinski the optician – Janek, not Krysztof. Krysztof Kozinski I haven't heard from for – what? – seventeen years or so now – in fact, not since that postcard from Vienna – the one with the picture of the opera house on the front and the absurdly blue skies. And, of course, that peculiar spidery writing of his. *Wish you were here. Where are the others? Did anyone else get out?*

Janek?

You know I always thought it was strange for a big man like Krysztof with such big hands to have such delicate handwriting.

Are you there? They said you wanted to talk –

You would have expected his writing to be dark and heavy –

Janek? Can you hear me?

The strokes of his pen as incorruptible and straightforward as his general character. But no: loops and swirls are all you get from Krysztof – loops and swirls.

Ten thirty-five

SILENCE.

Janek?

Nothing.

Son? Can you not hear me?

So then.

A chance to do some thinking.

A note to myself.

On the matter of Scott Fitzgerald and my forthcoming seminar, *In Search of the Green Light: Sexual Fantasy in Modern American Literature*, I must – simply *must* – this time not allow a repeat of last summer's incident –

Oh, it's so cold here, Janek –

Such carelessness – such blindness – is unforgivable in a man of my age –

And the others, well, they're so, so –

I am, after all, nearly forty-one years old; old enough (easily) to be her father (haha).

So . . . blinded, Janek. Janek? Are you there? Can you hear me, Janek?

Yes I can hear you

How could I not, when you persist so?
   But, son, it was you that had me woken!
   I think not.
   I think so.
   I think not.
   I think so.
   This is stupid.
   Early too.
   What?
   It's early. I should still be asleep.
   But you're dead.
   And you think we don't need sleep – what with all we have to do?
   I'm dreaming this.
   All the haunting and such –
   I said I'm dreaming –
   If you say so.
   Yes, I'm asleep and I'm dreaming.

I should be so lucky.

Oh God –

Oh, now don't drag Him into this –

What?

I said –

I heard what you said. Look, just leave me alone, will you?

But what about the river?

Fuck the river.

What?

And fuck you, too.

Nice. Your mother would be sooo proud.

What?

Not to mention your wife. The mother of my precious grandchild.

Don't mention Rachel. Don't you mention Rachel.

I will if I want. It's a free country.

Who told you that?

Haha. That's my boy!

Oh just fuck off, will you?

Yes. I might just do that.

Go ahead.

Right. But you'll want me back.

Have you gone yet?

Give me a chance.

I'm counting to three. One –

Oh, come on –

Two –

All right, all right –

One –

I'm going –

My big mistake

EVERYONE knows it's never pleasant to discover how predictable you are — how easily your mind can be read and your actions foretold. It is disempowering, making you believe, as it does, that you never really had any choice about things in the first place, and that, consequently, any notion you might have had of any personal sovereignty — of having had any degree of control over your own destiny — was really just foolish vanity. And *then*, of course, apart from serving to diminish yourself in your own eyes, it has the other consequence of making you come to despise whoever it was that revealed your shallowness in the first place — even if that person was one person who made living with the knowledge bearable.

So then, a paradox. You cannot win. The liberator as destroyer.

And so to Rachel: my wife and Ewa's mother.

You must have a crick in your neck, she'd say, *from all this searching behind you*, and she'd challenge me to say that not all good things are past, and that happiness need not always be retro-spective. She'd try to get me to say *I am happy* when I was (I never did) – to say it right then – *at that moment* – without fearing that in the challenge of naming it it would all just shrink away.

I am happy.

There's Americans for you.

I am happy right now.

There's Rachel for you.

Looking back now, I see it as bizarre (or ironic, or something) that it was because of Rachel – because of her insistence on daring to acknowledge the present in all its rawness before it takes on the safety of the past – that I made what is universally now (it seems) regarded as My Big Mistake. I mean, had it not been for such sound and caring advice, then surely I would never have lingered that fateful moment too long – that is, allowed myself to be swayed by the attentions and flattery of someone who, for all her familiar charm and precocious intelligence, was little more really than a child. Of course, I know now that for me to have attempted any kind of defence of my actions just served to make them appear even worse (as if, by defending myself, and therefore them, it was obvious that, despite what I said, I thought them in the end defensible, and so didn't *really* believe they were wrong at all) – but really, what else could I do? If I have learned nothing else in my life, then surely I've learned that truth is never served by silence, and that an innocent man is as guilty as the Devil if, by that silence, he allows injustice to prevail. And so, call me foolish or naive (and, believe me, I've already been called that and much, much more), but I really feel I had no choice but to speak out. Of course, that my so doing was to have quite the consequences it did, I could never have foreseen – and for that I am truly sorry. However, as I said to the committee, in the end I am not solely culpable and should therefore not be the one held solely to blame.

Yeah, right –

I am vulnerable too, I said – not unreasonably – and it was then I knew that I would at least to some degree survive. For I could see in their eyes that, despite all their bluster and outrage, they really *needed* me to survive, for without this they would have to have considered the validity of their own survival – and which one of them could possibly have survived *that*? And so, in the end, I suppose you could say that justice, in a manner of speaking, was served – particularly since there remains for me still the at least theoretical possibility of being able to clear my name through the university's laborious appeals procedure, although, of course, I have few illusions about the likely chances of success if this current action goes against me. Mud, after all, as they say, sticks – and some kinds of mud worse than others. I mean, even now, well before I've exhausted such possibilities of redress open to me, there are the *looks* – looks that I know will never, whatever happens, go away. They are the looks of disgust on the faces of the men (disgust, for I am publicly what they know themselves secretly to be), and – on those of the women – exhaustion, what with my still-possible (albeit slim) survival being just the latest in a long line of defeats.

But then, in the end, I suppose looks are nothing. Sticks and stones. Maybe, in the end, survival is enough. Even for the hungry like me.

I think you mean guilty.

What?

You said hungry. I think you mean guilty.

Oh, I do, do I? Well, for that matter, I think *you* meant *hot.*

What?

When you said a while back how cold it is where you are. I think you meant hot.

But I am cold.

But – excuse me – I thought it was supposed to be hot down there?

Well it isn't.

OK. Whatever.

What does that mean?

Nothing. It means nothing. Look, are you planning on wasting much more of my time like this?

Why? What are you going to do?

I don't know. All I know is this is stupid.

What's stupid?

This.

Well you started it.

No I didn't.

Yes you did.

Exactly *how* did I start it?

You woke me up.

I *what?*

You woke me up. I was sleeping. Minding my own business.

Minding your own business?

And trying to stay out of your way.

Well you should have tried a little harder.

I could go now if you like.

Good.

Then shall I?

Yes.

Not that it'll make a difference.

Oh, it'll make a difference all right. Believe me.

Whatever you say.

Well?

Well what?

I thought you were going.

I'm going.

So go.

All right then.

But one thing before I do

WHAT now?

Well, there's something I should check.

What?

Well —

Oh, for Christ's sake, get on with it, will you? There's things I have to do —

You promise you won't be angry?

Jesus Christ.

All right. Well, the thing is, I just need to check — just need to be sure — that you know who you're talking to.

I know.

You do?

I said I know. Now, will you let me get on?

And you don't mind?

Would it matter if I did?

Well —

I mean, if I said go away, would you?

Probably not.

Well then. Just be quiet, will you, and let me get on –

Yes of course.

Fine.

There's just one other thing –

What?

Ewa.

What about her?

Well, shouldn't she be back by now?

What do you mean?

I mean – oh, nothing. It's just, well, you said you were hungry.

So?

Well, it would be typical of her to forget now, wouldn't it?

Forget what?

Your lunch.

She won't forget.

If you say so.

I do. Now, is that all?

For now, yes.

Good.

Doubt planted, doubt grows

LORD, I can only hope she has remembered to pick up something for lunch. It's amazing how hungry just sitting around doing nothing can make you. Right now I'm starving. The last thing I ate was some of that cheap stringy ham at breakfast, and some cheese that should have been thrown out weeks ago. God, no wonder Ewa stays out more and more these days. I used to think it was perhaps what happened last summer that kept her away (from me) – but maybe I was wrong. Maybe it's just been the poor state of my housekeeping. There is, after all, scarcely anything more depressing than an empty fridge – anything more hopeless-looking – nor, of course, anything more cheering than a full one. Not that I actually remember the last time I had a full one, of course –

But anyway.

Lunch.

You know what I'd really like? What I'd really like is a McDonald's hamburger – or a cheeseburger, maybe, and one of those little apple pies that comes in a box. And French fries. And a drink. Coke. The Real Thing. I don't know what it is about that place, but I just love it. I even dream about it sometimes. When it's not my father and his screaming atonement, or Rachel and her beautiful hands, or a certain young lady and the way she used to hold her books before her like a shield, it's McDonald's that fills up my night hours – or, more precisely, McDonald's and me – *just* me – me and one of those cheap plastic trays piled high with food – so much food, in fact, that when I've eaten it all I at once start to vomit – covering my shirt-front and my trousers, and then the floor – and then always in my dream I can't stop vomiting – I just go on and on until I'm drowning, or until I wake up.

Which all means what?

To a psychoanalyst I suppose it would mean some kind of rejection – an effort on my part to rid myself of that which is vital to me. That or something. However, I am not a psychoanalyst, and will have nothing to do with what such a person would clearly come to see as some ridiculous and theatrical attempt at suicide. Oh no. Down that road lies a real kind of madness, and not just this stuff I've been faking. Down that road lie the bodies still of all my terrible errors, the presence there of which it has taken me years to accept and not to fear. So, right now (as Rachel would always advise), I shall not think of them. Right now, I shall think of the future and not of the past. I shall think about my daughter. *Our* daughter.

And Rachel – her mother.

Oh of course I shall think about Rachel.

The first time I saw her

She was standing, her head bowed, offering prayers in a place where so many had been offered – and so many ignored. I stood watching her for a while (I was on a break: just time enough for coffee and a cigarette), and in a while she raised her head – but slowly, as if she wore a heavy crown of stone. After a few minutes, she opened her eyes. Others around her were standing mute, some weeping, some taking pictures for their holiday albums. ('Here's me at the execution wall!' I always imagined them saying, or 'Just look at those latrines – how filthy they are! How unkempt!', and I'd think of them then sitting heavy at home on some over-stuffed couch, stubby fingers stabbing blunt at coloured photographs trapped under cellophane.)

It was only later, when (accidentally of course) I bumped into her in the café, that I discovered she was an American. And it was only as I was making some attempt to clean up the mess at her feet that I discovered her temper.

'Look, just leave it, will you?' she said.

To which, of course, I apologised.

She just turned away.

Rising then, I couldn't help noticing her ring. I mentioned her husband.

'What?' she said.

'He's not with you, then – your husband?'

That, she said, was none of my business. And, anyway, there *was* no husband. The queue moved on; so did she.

I followed.

'Yes, I'm sorry,' I said.

'You said that,' she said.

'It's a failing,' I said.

'What?' she said. She turned. Her eyes, I saw then, were more beautiful than any eyes I'd ever seen.

'Apologising,' I said. 'It's a failing. Personal. National. We just can't stop.'

She frowned, but behind the frown somewhere was a smile. 'Have you tried?' she said.

I nodded. 'Tried. Failed. Sorry.'

Briefly the smile flowered, then was gone.

'I love you,' I said then, but only in my head, and I believe, in her head too, but somewhere so far away and so deep, she said she loved me too.

Twelve noon

IT must be the gloom of this place (or maybe the gloom in my mind brought on by hunger), but I've just remembered an incident that happened a while ago at the university – something that I could not then and still can't explain. It was in the middle of the Easter break, and I was just going through some papers in my office, searching for (I think) some notes on a paper I'd been preparing on the novels of Thomas Wolfe, when I felt a kind of chill – the sort of chill you feel when you look round and find you're being studied by someone who wishes you harm. Well, of course, being a rational man, first of all I checked the windows, but found them tight shut and bolted. Then I put my hand to the heating grille in the wall – but nothing. Was there a draught coming in from under the door? I got down on my knees and checked. Again, nothing. So I dismissed it as just my mind playing tricks and got on with my searching.

Anyway, an hour or so must have passed then, when I felt

the chill again, and again I felt a strong sense of being watched. Again I went to the window. I scoured the old courtyard as best I could (the glass is old and uneven and so buckles and twists any image viewed through it), but could see nothing – no figure half hidden behind a pillar or the shape of a man in the shadows. So I turned away – back into the room – telling myself not to be such a fool. I am, after all, just a professor – not a spy – and have no secrets the presence of which would require special spy-type skills to reveal.

So. Again I settled down to my work. But I couldn't concentrate. I kept thinking that if there was nothing in the courtyard, then there had to be something in the room itself. But what? It never was a large room and there aren't many places to hide. Anyway, feeling rather foolish, I got down on my hands and knees and checked under my desk. Here all I discovered was several years' worth of dust. So I got up and brushed myself down. I looked behind the bookcase that juts out halfway across the room – but of course nothing. I was stumped – so much so that I was ready to call off the search when I heard a noise like footsteps coming from the corridor. Suddenly frozen, I stood listening. The footsteps stopped. I crept to the door and twisted the handle with one hand, reaching with the other for my ever-flowerless vase. I eased the door open and peered outside.

Nothing.

Nobody.

Then another noise – this time more distant – footsteps again, growing fainter. I followed, holding tight for dear life to the vase. Rounding the corner, then, I swear my eye caught something – movement – something dark and swirling, a pair of shapes disappearing like the fleeing tails of an old-fashioned frock-coat. 'Hello?' I said, aware of a trembling in my voice. No answer. I headed slowly along the hall to the corridor's next turn. Here I eased my back to the wall like you see American policemen do on TV, and tried to regulate my breathing. I closed my eyes and counted to ten. Then, with little or no care for how foolish I might appear, I launched myself around the corner, screaming AAAAH! at the top of my voice as I went.

Well.

As it turned out I needn't have bothered. For what did I find? Some unshaven threatening menace? Some ghoul raised in bad humour from the grave?

Of course I found nothing. No one. All there was was the usual end-of-term silence and stillness. No giveaway footprints leading off into some unseeable, unknowable distance, no trace in the air of some mysterious perfume. Just that out-of-season limbo – that, and further confirmation, of course, that what Rachel had said that had hurt so much at the time was in fact quite true: that if I didn't change my ways and fast then I'd end up all alone with no one to betray now and abuse but myself.

Oh she was hard sometimes, Rachel.

Hard but probably fair. After all, look at me now. I am truly a man obsessed. With what? Oh, I am too ashamed to say – too embarrassed to admit just how many of the university's hours I have spent at my computer, both appalled and aroused by what I can so easily find. I am too ashamed to admit just how easily this absurd and disgusting technology has caught me in its grip. I am a weak man – I know that now, and I am sinking fast.

And yet, and yet, despite everything, I still feel (why I could not say) that there is something enduring inside me that nothing – not even the worst and most perverse degradation – can entirely destroy.

At least, ladies and gentlemen, this is my hope. It is my hope that all chance of redemption has not finally been lost, and that should such an undeserved opportunity suddenly appear before me I will not be so blind that I cannot see it, nor so cowardly that I will not dare to wager what is left of my soul for the chance – for the first time in years – of finally sleeping soundly again in a bed not cursed with the squalling, misshapen, poisoned fruit of lies.

Ewa

I'VE been thinking some more now about the manner of Ewa's leaving, and it occurs to me that I may have made something of a strategic error in trying to please her as I did (or, as she would see it, in trying, through a gift, to win my way back into her good thoughts), and that I should perhaps have just let sleeping dogs lie. But just doing nothing – just waiting for enough time to pass – is sometimes so hard, particularly when you've been faced every morning over breakfast by the face of someone whom you so dearly love but who seems now to have nothing left in her heart for you other than barely disguised contempt.

I know, I know. Believe me, I know.

Not, you understand, that I could – or do – blame her. On the contrary. How could I? If a man cannot forgive his own trespasses, then how, in heaven's name, can he expect forgiveness from others?

One thirty-seven

WELL, the street is beginning to quieten down again after the lunchtime rush. The flower-sellers in the square have started culling their blooms, weeding out and shedding those that have wilted, tossing them back into the boxes from which, around dawn, they'd emerged. You know, ever since I was a boy I've always found this a scene of such infinite sadness, speaking as it does of the brevity of even this, the most harmless, the most selfless, form of life.

Son, do you remember that sailing boat? The one your grandfather made?

But then, as people say, there's always tomorrow. Except, of course, when there isn't –

I remember your face, and how you just couldn't wait for the weekend –

You know, people don't seem to realise that those fools who walk around proclaiming that today – that *right now* – is the moment of the end of the world will one day be proved right, or that the man who, every day, tells you he's dying and that he'll scarcely survive another hour, will, in the end, one day, be seen to have been telling the truth –

Janek? Don't you remember?

No, we all live lives of wilful and selective blindness – for, if we didn't, how could any one of us bear to draw the morning curtains or close our eyes at night, knowing that today could be our last day and that, if it is, everything unresolved will stay unresolved, and that a man and, say, his daughter will remain disunited – that that which should keep them together for ever – those precious ties of family – will never be repaired and the bonds for ever broken –

Janek?

Oh, but listen to me whining so, when, for me, for sure, there is a tomorrow. For me, for now, all that I have done I can still undo, and all that I have not done I can at least try to do.

Starting with Ewa's return.

Don't you remember how its sails would fill out at the merest breath of wind?

If she returns.

But no – I shall not think like that. For heaven's sake, what would her mother have said about such hopeless defeatism? No. I shall wait, watch and listen. I shall sit here and study the street until she appears, and then, when I hear that door close and the sound then of her rising footsteps, I shall ready myself. I shall stand in this window, with our city behind me, and tell her that she cannot go on punishing me for something for which I have already been punished – that she must forgive me, otherwise –

But no. As I said, there is a place I must not go. There is a place I must leave for another day. For the moment, I must stay positive – for the moment I will stay positive, I will, I will, I will.

But then a few minutes pass and

WELL, I must have been imagining things when I thought I heard the latch drop a moment ago. She's probably still hanging about with that so-called friend of hers and getting up to God-knows-what – all of which is just one more thing I don't want to think about right now. All I want to think about right now is what I should be thinking about, and what I should be thinking about is work.

In Search of the Green Light.

What was originally meant to be the title of a whole series of lectures on the theme of sexual fantasy in modern American literature will now, I suppose, have to suffice as the title of just one written paper – a paper which I intend (despite whatever objections there might be from the faculty – particularly Dean Nowak and his snivelling sidekick Kubicka) to submit to the quarterly journal of the American Cultural Institute in Warsaw. Of course, should they accept it for publication, well, that would be sweet indeed, although sweeter still would be an invitation to speak at the biannual convention next spring. Oh, I can just imagine their faces now. There they'd be, the two of them representing this fine old university of theirs (I used to think of it as mine too – but that's all long gone now), sitting there in their cheap suits in that great draughty auditorium, having to listen to the words of a man they've tried so hard to discredit, and all because, when it came down to it, they revealed themselves to be utterly spineless – entirely without that unbending, incorruptible moral strength about which they have long been making such a fuss.

But I mustn't get carried away.

First things first.

First, there is all that work to do. Which I'm not going to get done at all if all I do is sit here worrying about Ewa.

So stop worrying is what I must do.

Except I can't.

O Lord, am I just being some wretched over-protective father by saying that she seems far too young to be even going out with boys – let alone *sleeping* with them? God, I hardly dare imagine what Rachel would say were she here now, what with me being (and obviously having *been*) so lax in the discipline department.

But then she's not here.

So – for good or ill – it's all down to me.

But what precisely should I do? What, now, *can* I do? How, after the events of last summer, can I expect her to listen to a word I say? It's bad enough that I should have set such a bad example for my daughter, without the object of that example having been so close to home.

All of which is not helping with the matter in hand, which is what to do about the situation when Ewa eventually decides to return. Of course, what I shall probably do is nothing (why break the habit of a lifetime?), when I should, of course, just put my foot down. Once and for all. Just say no. Just tell her she's too young and too pretty to be throwing herself away. Just stand here and tell her straight. Just tell her I love her and have always loved her, and that I'm only thinking of her and her future.

Yes.

That's it.

Courage.

Conviction.

A problem solved.

All I need now is for the wretched girl to come home.

Waiting

WAITING, waiting, always waiting. Always sitting at some window, peering out, either hoping for or fearing an arrival.

And always, in the meantime, waiting.

Like waiting, already corrupted, in that cellar for the sound of a soldier's boots. Like sitting, already guilty and so quiet in the damp darkness that your thoughts seem to scream at you and will not let you rest. Like waiting, all those years ago – me, Fredzio, Borowski and Krysztof – before I knew about life all that I would come to know, before that which had seemed invincible was crushed by the weight of nothing heavier than wishes, and that which seemed so precarious prevailed, bringing with its survival the wretched curse of hope.

But enough talking in riddles.

In fact, enough talking.

I'm tired of talking, of thinking.

Perhaps I'll close my eyes.

Maybe sleep, maybe dream

BUT dream of what? Of whom?

Well, Rachel, of course.

'Because you like it here.'

Or maybe not.

'Because it makes you feel alive.' Isn't that what she said?

You know it is. In daydreams and dreams in the night.

Try to forget it.

You think I *haven't* tried? Believe me, I have. But every time I do – every time I turn away from the past and start looking forward – there she is again, barring my way, standing by my side so beautiful and so calm at that altar, or frowning at me (but smiling too) in that café queue at the camp.

You should learn to escape.

How? You mean like you? You mean by trading my skills for my freedom?

Not freedom. Survival.

Forget it. It's not that easy any more.

Easy? You think it was easy? You weren't there. You don't know.

Oh I was there all right. You saw to that. And now I'm here. And you say forget. You say escape. Well how *can* I escape – how *can* I forget – when that moment when your eyes met my mother's – that morning – was my very life's axis?

Calm down. You're getting hysterical.

– When later, as a consequence everything I did was just everything I did. When every morning, at the same time, I'd get up, then, every morning, eat the same breakfast, then walk the same route to the university. There – though every day was, in some ways, different – every day was also just the same as the day before and the one to follow – just another sequence of hours to be sat through in the same kind of low-battery daze. Even the muttered talk in the corridors and coffee-rooms – the group's plotting and fantasy – had from the very beginning (at least to me) come to seem nothing more than just that – plotting and fantasy. It all seemed to me to have about as much chance of turning into reality as I did of passing my finals with anything higher than a second. Which is not to say, of course, that I didn't indulge – we all did – but just that it never seemed real – even when it was Fredzio doing the talking. Even then – even as I, his faithful acolyte, stood, nodding, beside him (I would even hold his coat sometimes, to free up his arms for those sharp, slashing gestures of his that would so thrill his audience with their promise of blood) – even then I could feel myself wallowing quite careless in the luxury of forced inaction, never dreaming of course that the day would come when such lethargy, such indulgence of self, would no longer be an option – except to those (like me) to whom the pleasures of dreaming had always outweighed those of action and the day.

But then, in those bleak, draughty corridors, or hunched over like spies in those gloomy soulless rooms, I had as little belief in the inevitability of what we all see now as the inevitable future as I had understanding of the influence upon me – upon us all – of the inescapable past. Then, in those days, when a day slipped by and was gone from my sight, it instantly ceased to exist for me as profoundly as did the days that I knew in my head but could never really believe were surely to come. Then, in those days, each day as it spread out around me was all I could (or ever wanted to) see; then, in those days, the days were calm and empty. In those days, during term time especially, I hadn't anything to run to or anything pressing to escape from – nor – at least to start with – during the holidays, when, although it's true that everything changed, the change was from one dull and dulling routine to another: wake up, breakfast, out of the house and turn left instead of right; in my hand, instead of books, a bag of sandwiches, a piece of fruit. And then, instead of the walk across the square and under those famous arches, a ride for the best part of two hours on what has to have been the slowest and dirtiest (not forgetting the noisiest) bus in the whole of humanity – a ride that, every day, came to its same clanking, diesel-spewing end, with the driver's raised and grubby hand and his calling out, '*Oswiecim! Anyone for Oswiecim!*', followed, every day, by his grinning in the mirror as he informed the bus's complement that – for Jews and gentiles alike – Oswiecim, *Auschwitz*, was the end of the line.

Looking back, it amazes me now to think that scarcely once, during those days and summer weeks every year that turned into months, did it occur to me that perhaps I was there – leading those groups of children and grown-ups from the death wall to the gas chambers and on to my father's barracks and back, each place a time for pausing and retailing some grim and ghastly tale (not forgetting the opportunity for pictures) – not simply as a consequence of a form filled out correctly and good references as to character asked for and provided, but as the result of something more: some kind of attempt, perhaps, from without or within at a balancing act – a consequence, perhaps, of a wish or a need to resolve accounts outstanding from generations past and deeds by some forgotten – a need for a summing-up of the state of affairs, in order that a profit or loss might be declared and arrangements made to cover any short-fall. No. In those days – until the day I met Rachel and everything changed – everything, every day, was the same. Every day, in those days, before I knew – before I felt, and so knew without really *knowing* – that that bus-ride, every day, was for a part of me at least, always a bus-ride home – a journey back to my beginning – all I would see, when I pointed to those ovens or stood gazing down at the scars of the land where once, in deep pits, had been gathered the still-writhing bodies of the dead for burning, was a time so ancient and, conse-quently, foreign to me that it might just as well have been the time of some distant Mogul empire, or the time, long gone, when Europe's first Vandals had ravished the earth.

Is that it, then?

Oh, it's you again.

You've quite finished?

Fuck off.

Well, charming.

It wasn't meant to be. And anyway, I didn't ask you to listen in, did I?

How could I not?

Look. Just leave me alone, will you? This is not for you, anyway –

No? Then who?

They need to know things.

Things about me?

And other things.

You mean how I was such a bad father.

You said it.

I can't listen to this.

So don't.

Are you sure you want to do this?

I have to.

No you don't.

Yes I do.

Please.

Fuck off.

All right, all right. I'm going.

For good this time?

If that's what you want.

It is.

All right. Goodbye then.

And don't come back.

You'll regret this.

I don't think so.

You will. You'll see. You need me.

Look, I'm not listening to this any more. In fact, I'm too tired to go on with this right now.

Except to say this

EXCEPT to say that I remember, ladies and gentlemen, how my wonderful father would scold me every time I had an accident, how he would quietly instruct me to stand before him, exhibiting my shame, and how he'd not let me go – not let me rid myself of the stinking, stinging mess – until he was quite ready. I remember how he'd sit there in his chair, his eyes closed tight and a frown of such disgust on his face, until something inside him – some voice, I always used to think, that only he could hear – would tell him to release me, and he'd open his eyes and smile. 'There now,' he'd say, 'you just run along now,' and all, it seemed, would be forgotten – forgotten at least until the next time.

And there was always a next time. Always, sooner or later – and always with no warning – there I'd be, queuing for a tram, or waiting in the dark for the film to begin, when I'd feel the start of that slow, warm invasion.

Of course, when I grew older (but not, it shames me still to say, for some years out of this unfortunate habit) – when I grew more certain that everything has not only a consequence but a cause – I tried to think *why* – tried to work out what each circumstance had in common, so that maybe I could bear it stillborn – but, hard as I tried, I could never arrive at any likely conclusion. Until, that is, that something that I had been able neither to understand nor escape made me climb a set of dank wooden stairs in a building down by the river (a place whose narrow hall of darkness I can still remember as sweeping around me like some kind of velvet cloak), and then knock on a grubby yellow door.

Now, from this distance, all I see of her is the paleness of her face (a face, now as then, without features, without definition) – that, and the bitter, mocking tone of her voice. She hated me, of course, and of this I was glad. I was grateful that she clearly didn't see in me that which others claimed to see – my 'good qualities' as my mother called them – and that, consequently, I didn't have to feel guilty about 'disappointing myself'. That, despite such sound logic, I still *did* feel guilty says much, I suppose, about my character then (and probably now) – then (and probably now, I'm really too close to judge) my being quite unable to escape the savage judgements of those all around me, even when they were, quite clearly, unaware of my presence . . .

But I wander in my story.

Back to those stairs, that dark room.

Back to Irena.

She was sitting, I recall, on the end of a messed-up bed, her lank hair hanging forward and disguising her face, her gaze cast down upon a bundle in her arms. *Oh God*, I thought at once, *a baby*, and I thought of my mother and I tried to turn – tried to get away before she could see me – but my legs that had been so unsure beneath me as they'd climbed the stairs, bringing me to this rendezvous, now were as solid and immovable as ancient timber. So I could do nothing but just stand there, staring dumbly at the top of her head – at the pale zig-zag parting that divided the swathes of her hair – thinking only of the safety of my room and the darkness and protection there of my own narrow bed with the bloodless embrace of its clean cotton sheets.

She lifted her head.

'What do you want?' she said.

I felt myself shaking my head.

'You have money?'

I dropped my eyes from hers, unable to stand the precision of their gaze. In their sharpness they seemed to know me at once for who I knew myself to be, and so to hold for me nothing but contempt.

'I'm sorry,' I said.

'Sorry? For what?'

At last I managed to turn away.

'Where are you going?' she said.

My back to her, I took a step. The truth was I *was* sorry, although – as ever – I didn't know what for.

'Doesn't your wife know you're here?'

'What?' Another step.

'Or maybe you're late for school?'

School. Her voice, suddenly young-sounding now, was taunting. 'I don't go to school,' I said. 'I go to university.'

A whistle from behind me. 'Well now,' she said. '*That's* a different matter. And there was I thinking I'd got myself a schoolboy. There was I thinking I'd have to show you what to do –' A rustling, then, of bedclothes, the creaking of ancient springs. 'Well, *Mister* University,' she said, 'don't you want to take a look?'

Oh God, I felt sure I'd be sick. 'Look –' I said, though no further words came, as, in that very moment, as my chest started heaving, I creased double at the waist and watched as my vomit descended, heard it splatter on the bare wooden floor.

I woke sometime later, expecting to find myself in my bed back at home (indeed, so strong was this expectation, and so certain my belief that it had all been a dream, that on first opening my eyes, all around me was familiar – until, that is, what was sharp in my room began softening, the details blurring, until the room was replaced by another), only to find myself still where I'd left myself – still in a whore's room, still within the clutter and the gloom.

'So you're back then.'

Indeed, so dark was the room, its edges so lost in shadow, that there could have been an audience for what was to follow and I'd never have known – a crowd of human vipers looking on and smiling with cynical disgust.

'Better now?'

A hand touched my brow. It was warm and soft – a child's hand, it felt like. I pushed up; my head was pounding.

'You want something to drink?'

I turned, searched the darkness for the source of the voice, for the body attached to the hand. Nothing. Just vague, formless shapes. I squinted hard. Slowly, then, one by one, the shapes coalesced into furniture – a table, a basin, a lamp on a tall spindly stand.

'Well, do you?'

And then – somewhere far off in what seemed to me like a corner – a figure emerged – a head, shoulders, the arms of a chair.

'What time is it?' I said. My voice was muffled, as if I were speaking through a wall of cotton-wool.

The figure in the corner moved – a shrug. '*I* don't know,' she said. A pause, breathing. 'Don't you have a watch?'

I shook my head: my watch – a gift from my parents – had been lost – lent to Fredzio and never returned.

Another shrug, followed by a moment's stillness, during which, my eyes having grown slowly accustomed to the low-light, I made out the limbs, head and torso of another body – this time the body of a child. The child (the same child, I assumed, that before she'd been cradling in her arms) now was naked, its arms and legs stiff, its eyes wide and gleaming, unblinking. I looked hard at the strange, inert thing, searching for some – any – sign of life; evidently, she took exception to my staring for, in a hard, cynical tone, she said, 'And what are *you* looking at, eh? Haven't you ever seen a baby before?'

A doll, I thought suddenly, and with some great relief, *it's only a doll*.

But then, as if she'd heard my thoughts and wished to make of me a fool by proving them wrong, the woman in the shadows stretched out her leg and jabbed the figure on the floor with her toe. The figure moved lumpenly – heavy and reluctant like a body in sleep or death.

'Oh my God,' I said, unable to stop myself.

The rustling of clothing; the woman leaned forward. In the light's coarse relief, her face, I could see, was pale and pitted. She shook her head, although smiling incongruously. 'God?'

she said, mocking. 'You see how he killed my baby and you still believe in God?'

I opened my mouth, intending to say something – to repeat that pathetic form of words in God's defence that for so long had been drummed into me by my mother – but nothing would come – just the knowledge in that moment of my own ridiculous desire and arousal.

A sigh from across the room; the woman leaned back into shadows. In a while she said, 'So you want to fuck me?' Her voice, almost a whisper now, held trapped within it – somewhere as far back perhaps as childhood – a shallow note of pleading.

I swallowed hard, heard the dry click of my throat.

'Well?' she said.

And so I nodded, and so she stood, and, stepping over her baby with a mother's casual care, she lay with me in the darkness on her whore's narrow bed, our limbs in their movement lit only by the twin failing lights of conscience and despair.

Two fifteen

THE first time I read that line in Durrell, the one in which he writes of events overlapping each other 'like wet crabs in a basket', I knew he was writing exclusively for me. I knew because – even in childhood, when things are supposed to be so straightforward – so uncomplicated – but never are (ask any child) – I could always feel, with each new thing learnt, the slithering of those crabs drawing over me in battalions, one then another and another, until there was nothing above me – no sight of the sky – nothing but the hardness of their shells all around me and their salt-smelling flesh, and the clicking like knives of their sharpening claws.

Not that I ever shared this with anyone.

Not, ladies and gentlemen of the jury, that is until now.

And why now?

Well. Along, to be fair, with the wise Mr Sikorski, I suppose I just thought it might help things along. And anyway, who is left, besides me, to be troubled by such revelations of (I suppose) childhood trauma? No one is who. Just me. And this is all just stuff *I* already know.

No.

Those people who should hear it – should have heard it – are long gone now.

But what about Ewa? you say. Is she gone too?

Well, as good as. As good as. And anyway, I said *people*, didn't I?

I did, yes.

Except I should have said person.

And yes, you know you know who. He who made me the man I am today. He who was never honest until the moment of his death – and only then because of cowardice, only then because fear of God's anger demanded it. You see, only then, in that last hour of life, did he call me – his son – to his side and bequeath me the truth – hand it on to me like so much poisoned fruit. Only then, at the first touch of death's embrace, when all that for so long has been struggled for is nearly lost and a man is free of cursing, did he tell me his story that was my story too. And only then did I understand what Thomas Wolfe meant when he said that you can't go home again; what he meant, I knew then (and I know still today), was that the very act of leaving – of taking that journey – changes for ever the place from which you departed, just as, with the whistle at last and the movement of the train, so, too, is the station in motion, moving back and away in the only way that counts, which is in a person's memory, the place, once so familiar, left suddenly bereft, abandoned to that muffling of overlapping time.

Yes yes, you say, this is all very well, but what did he *say*? What could he *possibly* have said that could have been so important?

Well . . .

Come on! you say. *Come on!*

Oh for God's sake don't hurry me. Is it you in the dock? Surely the accused can be given at least a little time to compose himself. I mean, have any of you ever faced such a thing?

Precisely.

So.

Once we've all quite settled down, I shall begin.

First, though, ladies (and some of you gentlemen), a word of caution. What you are about to hear will no doubt make you weep – being, as it is, one of the funniest things you'll ever have heard. So. Be prepared. Equip yourselves with tissues, and whatever else you'll need to get you through. For my part, I recommend vodka – although, at a guess, I'd say strong liquor is probably something you'll not be allowed – interfering as it does with a person's sober judgement.

Anyway.

The point is *don't ever try to tell anyone you weren't warned, OK?*

OK. Enough said.

Now. Where was I?

Oh yes.

My father.

My father on his death-bed.

My father on his death-bed, me, and my father's terrible secret.

My father who aren't in heaven

My father.

Yes. My father.

But where to begin?

At the end, perhaps, with sleep. Thus.

He never could sleep in the afternoons. At least not properly.
Not in a restful way. All he seemed able to do was to give up
the reins of this world just to take up those of another, harder
one.

Oh and then there were the dreams. Or rather, the *dream* –
for it was always the same. Always he was walking in a long
drawn-out group, heading for some schoolhouse in the country, always stubbing his toes and stumbling on the hard, frozen
ground. It was always winter, and all around him nothing but
silence – nothing, that is, but the sounds of shuffling figures and
the barking now and then – '*Raus! Raus!*' – of the teachers.
Sometimes they'd come to a ditch or some broken-down fence
and each one of them would have to make his or her way

across, picking over the rubble or the spikes, careful not to tear their precious uniforms for fear of some terrible although always unspecified retribution. And always there was this numb feeling – and not just from the cold, which was biting; no, it was another kind of numbness – this one coming from the inside out. It was like the kind of numbness that comes over a person when the last of that person's spirit has finally drained away, leaving him then just a slow-moving, stumbling corpse, careless now of the stones and their raising again of old wounds that have long since given up any struggle to heal.

And that was it – the dream. Of course, just exactly where it came from I could only, for a long time, speculate – and never with any kind of accuracy. All I knew was that it was waiting for him every time he closed his eyes at night – every night just the same. Every night there was always the same journey – the teachers (for so they always appeared) and their shouting, the children and their slipping on the icy ground, the mingling breath rising in the chill air like smoke from a chimney – always the stumbling, always the harsh, biting cold – always all this, but never the journey's end. Not once did they ever actually enter the schoolhouse. Before they did, he always woke up, amazed and appalled to find his heart beating still and the blood of life flowing hot and strong through his veins. And then always, in that strange hazy nowhere that exists like some airlock between dreams and the day, he'd start thinking again of the girl – my mother to be – at the window – of her pale, solemn face, and of the hopelessness and terror locked within it – and of how, lately, she'd even stopped screaming, withdrawing instead into the mute, depthless numbness of absence.

But look at me going on so – and about *dreams*, for heaven's sake – when there are so many other things to say, so many more *important* things – things like why is Ewa taking so long with her errand? And why, after so many years, must my father still creep out of his grave to be with me like this – and why *now* of all times – now when I've a shame quite the equal of his, and one that I fear will finish me any day now, just as surely as the schoolroom in the end finished him, leaving him with nothing but the sound in his ears of that terrible shrieking and stripping of flesh and the pain of feet so frozen from that petrified earth that nothing could ever warm them again and nothing stop the pain but the blessed relief of the surgeon's sharpest knife.

On the subject of which (feet, that is, not knives), my recent obsession with the pursuit of the truth (haha) obliges me to mention one last thing with regard to that dream – before it (like so much else these days) disappears from my nowadays unpredictable mind and is gone for ever.

And that thing would be?

Like I say, feet.

My father's in particular. Or – more particularly still – the foot (his left) he lost as a consequence of those ghastly winter walks.

Or not.

I should explain.

You see, as a boy (and I suppose this is natural – at least for such a solitary friendless child), however many times my father lied to me, I still, every time – every time he came up with a new and even more outrageous embellishment to the story – believed *this* version to be the true one (or at least *mostly* true, as complete truth seemed to me even then to be the preserve of God and His angels), and something from which some important lesson could probably be learned. For example, I believed him when he told me that his grandfather had been a rich man and a confidant of Louis Napoleon, but had lost all his money when the Second Empire fell, when in fact he'd been nothing more elevated than a driver of trams – and, later, I believed him – at least for a while – when he told me the tale of what had happened to his foot.

His foot.

Lord.

Just thinking about it now, sitting here – just closing my eyes and trying to imagine how many times he must have clumped up those steps, his face contorted with the effort, to find me then as I am today, my back to the window overlooking the street and my head buried deep in some book – just thinking about it now, I can't any longer understand why I didn't find a better hiding-place sooner – or at least learn sooner than I did that lesson about liars and the truth, and how it's only the little lies – not the big ones – that will always trap you for sure. But the fact is, for whatever reason, I didn't. Every time, I'd just lower my book and watch him as he made his awkward, old man's way around all this junk – knowing, as he did so, that I was in for another retelling of his fanciful, ludicrous, unbelievable (except, of course, to *me*) story. I'd brace myself then, waiting for the moment when he'd drop down beside me, his weight on the floorboards rattling the loose glass in the windows and raising the dust around my legs. '*Well now*,' he'd say, and for a moment then there'd be silence (my chance, I always used to think, to start the talk on some other topic – bikes or school, *anything* – a chance, though, never taken, as a freeze would come over me, stopping my voice in my throat), but then, sure enough, he'd stretch out his legs and point, sighing, at the absence. Then he'd say, '*Did I tell you what happened to my foot?*', and I'd find myself shaking my head, as surely doomed in that moment as any cavalryman faced with Panzers on the plains.

As for the story itself, though it was always different, it was always essentially the same – a tale of bad fortune, then a battle against the odds – a story of courage, of heroism, the triumph of will in adversity.

Not that, towards the end, I could still say I believed it – the story – for I came to know, instinctively somehow, that the truth lay elsewhere. It lay – the truth – I became certain of it – somewhere on that twice-daily march from the camp and back – somewhere between where he'd really come from and where he was really going. It was something concealed, a destination as yet unreached. Of this I was sure.

Later, when I knew it all – knew everything he'd no choice for his sanity's sake but to hide – there was still one thing I didn't understand – one mystery I really needed help with. I didn't understand why, year after year – even after more than forty years – he insisted on clothing the whole thing in fancy dress – why, for example, the teachers in his story were still always teachers (and he never one of them) and the children in the crocodile never the wretched living corpses they really were, their hides preserved, doomed to die. And the girls in the schoolhouse: why had they never aged into hopeless ragged whores? This I didn't understand – and still, in a way, don't. I mean, *surely* it's always better – isn't it? – to expose things to the air, to the spotlight of scrutiny – especially *bad* things – rather than to preserve them unchallenged in the darkness of the mind's stinking vault? Well, *isn't* it? Surely a man in the end *must* stand and face things – surely he can't keep *on* running – not for ever?

Or maybe he can.

Maybe he should.

Again I don't know.

Maybe if you keep on running long enough you'll eventually tire out your pursuer. Maybe, in the end. And maybe in the end *they'll* not bury *you* at all, but *you'll* be the one standing by a grave and weeping. Maybe. Maybe not. Whatever – either way – what's for sure is you'll never find out unless you've the courage to stand still, turn round, and face without running, without flinching, whatever is chasing you, and so give yourself a chance to remain, for a while at least, undefeated in the face of the past's infernal tide.

Three o'clock

AND the bells. Always the bells. The trumpeter, still warning of the tartar's advance.

Three o'clock.

Ordinarily by now – this being a Thursday – I'd just be finishing the last of the day's tutorials, signing off with some kind of a youthful flourish (or so I used to think), in an effort (doomed – I see that now) to persuade us both – my student and I – that the gulf of age and culture that our respective positions insisted lay between us was, in fact, just some outdated scholastic conceit, and that *really, underneath,* we were all the same.

Well.

Could I *really* have been so foolish? Did I *really* never see the mocking in their eyes as I brought out my well-rehearsed opinion of some ghastly new record?; or the looking away and laughter at my mention of some new club in town? Oh, how come I didn't see? Could I *really* have been so self-deluding?

It seems I could.

It seems I was.

It seems that somehow I convinced myself that they were all, *underneath*, just like *her*: that, *underneath*, they too – all of them – if they could only get to know *the real me* – would, like her –

Yeah, right –

– see as nothing the difference in our ages –

As if you weren't deluding yourself?

– and let me into their loud-mouthed, confident, hopeful world – the world from which time and ageing had so cruelly shut me out.

But, of course, with that ghastly, unsparing clarity of youth, they all saw me for precisely that which I am.

Exactly.

All but *her*.

Jesus –

Or so I thought. I thought (oh, how embarrassing this is to recount) that *she* was different – that *she* at least forgave me for the sin of trying to deny advancing age, and that, when my hand reached out and found its way beneath the hem of her dress, she neither flinched nor ran away nor uttered a single word of disapproval only because she *wanted* me to – because she, like me, saw and was scared by the terrible brevity of things – because she, too, saw how quickly and terminally the *now* in our lives turns to dust.

But of course I was wrong. It turned out that, even to *her* (she who knows me so well), I was just some curious specimen in a jar – a primitive example of expiring life to be teased and provoked into some kind of blind but wholly significant, proof-laden reaction, only then to be tossed aside, dumped, cast into the flames of this great, ever-burning, ever-burning –

Ever-burning what? Crematorium?

No, that would be in bad taste.

Let me just say *incinerator*. Or maybe *brazier*. Above all, let me not say . . . *that word* . . . for who knows who is listening? Who knows whose ears are burning (there's another bad word), or how far a (dead) man can hear these days, and, consequently, how careful those of us still living must be to not let any cats out of bags, or (God forbid) the truth crash this party of lies . . .

But there I go again.

It seems I cannot leave it alone.

I cannot, it seems, resist this temptation.

So.

Tell me.

Did I tell you the one about the old man and the school-house?

I didn't?

Or the bargain that was made – the secret shared of life and of death?

Ah well.

Well maybe I will and maybe I won't.

First, though – either way – let me tell you the one about the Russian, the East German and the Pole.

Are you ready?

Good.

Then I shall begin.

Three men go to heaven. At the gates they meet Saint Peter. Saint Peter tells them that they may ask him one question before they enter. Well, the Russian steps up. 'Sir,' he says, 'what will happen to Russia in the future?' Saint Peter thinks a minute, then leans forward and whispers his answer in the Russian's ear. 'Oh no!' cries the Russian, and begins to weep.

Next, the East German steps up. 'Sir,' he says, 'what will happen to the glorious GDR in the future?' Again, Saint Peter stands a moment in thought, then leans forward and whispers his answer. 'Oh no!' cries the East German, and he, too, begins to weep. Well, then comes the Pole. 'Sir,' he says, 'what will happen to Poland in the future?' For the third time, Saint Peter is lost in thought. Then, looking at the Pole, he begins to weep.

A joke to please surely even the Pope, my father's friend. Which makes me wonder. (This is not the first time.)

Did my father ever tell Uncle Karol any of his hilarious camp anecdotes?

I think you mean school.

Oh, hello.

I can't stand inaccuracy.

I'm glad you're here.

You are? I told you you would *be –*

Because now you can tell me – tell *us* – what *did* the Holy Father say when you told him your stories? Was he forgiving where I am not? Or was there, perhaps, just an awkward silence, what with the joke (however you take it) being evidence (as if more were needed) that the Church, these days (these days and all days, surely), is now about as useful as a professor, say, without a department . . .

But I ramble.

Back to that building at the camp that had once – it's true – been a schoolhouse.

No.

Only teasing!

You'll not get it out of me *that* easily. It would be wrong, surely – disloyal, even – to give up with so little fight that which another has fought so long to keep concealed. No. For *that* you'll have to wait. And maybe a long long time. For that, in fact – for the details of the drama you so seem to crave – you may have to wait until the actors are gone – every one of them – until enough time has passed to turn lives into history, and history into nothing more hurtful than fading photographs and dates.

Dates like December 13th 1981

TRULY, this, a date to remember.

Or to maybe forget.

Or maybe, at least, be a little tactful – a little discreet – in the remembrance of.

But, then, I am a dead man now anyway – so what does a little indiscretion matter? Just think of me, ladies and gentlemen, as William Holden in *Sunset Boulevard* – lying face down, a corpse in a swimming pool – dead, but somehow still able to tell the story of my demise.

Except, of course, that it's not *my* story – not really. For I, too, am (was) just an actor – an empty vessel given direction and lines by another – and scarcely any latitude with either, so that, should I stumble – should I forget where I am or who I am – I can blame someone else for that stumbling, for the humiliation heaped upon me as I stammer like a schoolboy and wish myself swallowed up and buried deep where no man, however earnest in his searching, would ever find me.

And I do.

Blame another, that is.

And not, I feel, without reason.

I blame him for my silence and for my whispered words on that day; I blame him, too, for the coward he'd made of me, and the martyrs, consequently, he made me make of others; I blame him for the hours spent fake and breathless in that cellar, and the oncoming, inaudible bootsteps of soldiers; I blame him for the river, then, and for the tides that wash away, and the gargoyles in the castle and their staring, demon eyes; but most of all, I blame him for bequeathing me the weakness that made breaking free of him impossible – that same weakness, that same terror at an undeclared future, that had made his own imprisonment so final – that had led him to that road, to that ice and those wretched shuffling souls – those men and women and above all the children – children whose flesh, despite the hopeless, searing cold, had held within it still the abundant warmth of life, and whose skin – though pale and near-bloodless now – was as clear, still, and unmarked as it had been when such times as these had seemed nothing more than rumour – when those afternoons and mornings, so long gone now, had seemed as endless and enduring as the cobbles in the square –

But enough, enough.

Yet again I wander. Yet again I let the neatness and pleasure of words overtake me – which indulgence, it occurs to me now (and, curiously, *only* now), being one reason why I never made a writer – just a man who talks about writing.

Others' writing.

Ah well.

I suppose we can only do in this life that for which fate has

prepared us, and hope that whatever it is we can be forgiven –
by our Church, by our country, by those who stand beside us,
by ourselves, by those still to come.

Speaking of whom.

Do you hear what I hear?

Yes I hear it.

You do?

As clear as day.

You're sure now?

Certain. But –

But what?

Shouldn't you be standing?

Standing?

You said you'd be standing when you faced her.

What? Faced who?

You know who.

You mean Ewa?

*I mean Ewa. Of course I mean Ewa. Who else is there? Who else is
still able to return?*

All right then. See, I stand.

Yes, but –

What now?

You really shouldn't look so pleading.

So how should I look? I feel like pleading.

You should be what you are.

Which is?

A man, of course.

Of course. Of course. A man.

Wrong again

FOR isn't a man more than just flesh and bone – more than such strength as this, more than this desire? Isn't a man a moral being, selfless and brave – a creature not swayed and corrupted by the gift of mortality?

You're rambling.

For if not this, then he is nothing. He is they and they are him, and there is no hope for either.

You're drunk.

I wish I were.

You must be.

What?

To have thought that was the door when it was obviously nothing of the sort.

I didn't.

You did. I felt it in our heart.

Oh Lord.

Jesus – Him again.

Maybe I'm losing my mind. I mean, you'd think by now I could pick out the sound of my own street-door opening — isolate it from all the other casual and deafening detritus —

It's an easy mistake.

But such, I suppose, is the hideous distortion heaped upon a person's senses by the power of wishful thinking.

Come on now. Cheer up.

Not that I could really claim to be *that* surprised at Ewa's continued absence. Harsh words *were* spoken — and not just about those scruffy hopeless types she hangs around with.

So there was more?

Well, yes. There was Henry James, for one.

Henry who?

James. Henry James.

Right.

You know, looking back on it now, I'll admit it still seems incredible to me that, despite all those years of school (not to mention being the daughter of an English professor — and a professor of American literature, for God's sake), she still (or so she claimed) has no idea who he was — has never heard of *The Wings of the Dove* or *The Europeans* or *The Golden Bowl*, and — worse than that — couldn't seem to care less. Of course, equally incredible to me now is the fact that I should have made such a fuss about it (what, after all, is the use of transmitting when there's no receiver — nobody to listen?), and particularly now, when there's still all this other stuff hanging over me — all these matters that are still unresolved. I mean, for heaven's sake, if any time to pick a fight was more likely to send her off down that street towards God-knows-where then I cannot now think of it. And anyway, it's not as if I could really claim to care any more about the House of Fiction and so on and blahblahblah —

at least, not in the way I used to. You know (incredible this) I used to think – to really *believe* – that art in the end was all that really mattered – that it actually had something valuable to teach us, and that in time of crisis we could turn to the works of great artists and find revealed there some blueprint for survival – some path which once taken would lead us out of this darkness and into the light of day.

Used to.

Not any more.

Not for some time have I been able to look at the spines of all those books in my study without disgust, without the sure and certain knowledge that if they really *do* have any message for us – some store of wisdom within them drawn from the sum of accumulated experience – then it is surely lost so deep in a language now so impenetrable that it might as well not be there at all.

Which thought, I can tell you, is not good for a professor of literature. For if the master no longer has faith in the lesson he's teaching, how can his pupils not reject it? How can they sit there any longer in silence making neat little notes in their books when they know what is being taught them is nothing short of useless? The answer is they cannot, as mine could not. As my pupils have begun to, they must start to look elsewhere for the lessons of life, for they surely cannot find them in the words of some long-dead American. No, if anywhere, they must learn what I have only just begun to learn: that is that books, in life, are less useful than tram tickets, that the canvas of paintings would be better used for tents, and that the only music worth hearing (but oh so seldom heard – especially in *this* house) is the sweet and solemn music of the truth.

That's the truth, Papa, the truth. *Papa?*

He's not here.

What?

I said he's not here.

Then who are *you*?

It doesn't matter.

This is crazy.

He said he had to go and lie down.

Lie down?

He said you were tiring him out.

Oh, well that's just great, isn't it. *I'm* tiring *him* out. That's just typical.

There's no need for bad feeling.

Oh, there isn't, is there? Well, *Papa*, if you can hear me now – now that – God help me – I'm turning into you, I hope you're satisfied. Now that my own child has turned away from me just as I turned away from you, I hope you can sleep as I can't. Oh I hope you can see what you've done – all that you left behind –

Sssh, now –

What?

Well, you'll wake everyone up –

Who? You mean the *dead*?

We prefer to think of ourselves as 'the sleeping'. The term doesn't have about it that spurious ring of absence. I mean, it's not as if we're out of reach –

Oh God.

Well now, there's a subject.

Oh, enough, enough. I know I know the dead are gone and I know they can never return –

Janek, darling?

Rachel? *Rachel?*

142

Sorry. Only kidding. A cruel joke, I know. Such facility with voices has got me into trouble before. For example: Hello? Are you still there? Janek? Can you hear me, Janek?

Oh yes I can hear you

EVEN in dreams.

Even as I stand here again with Rachel and our child (she still unborn, still just a whisper of some future to come) – the three of us here at this window overlooking the street, the rising stink of diesel seeping through the cracks. *I must go*, I am saying, but still I stand firm, my legs unwilling, my breathing short, my chest gripped tight at the sickening thought of danger. *I must go, I must go*, I say again, then again, and my voice starts to echo, and I know I will not go, but then I'm turning – *being* turned, ghostly hands on my shoulders – and then walking, gliding, a dream within a dream, my collar turned high, my frozen hands deep in my pockets, fingers searching for warmth but not finding it and only finding it in the heat from the street-corner brazier and the harsh looks of disgust and pity then of the soldiers who are really only boys but seem so much older so weary already do they look and so scrawny-necked and pale in their great-collared great coats and the way they stamp their feet so, like they're punishing the cobbles for nothing more than being cobbles, and then and then *Hey where were you?* says the officer, *I didn't think you were coming well I nearly didn't* says I (already hating myself even more for my complicity and him for leading me to it, for showing me the way), and there's snow on the peak of his cap like snow on a window-ledge and he's cupping his gloved hands and breathing steam through his fingers and then I hear a voice oh Lord it must be mine and then I'm crouching in a cellar and waiting and waiting and waiting just a bead in the living breathing rosary but a bead that's rotten if you can have rotten beads well even if you can't that's what I am and more waiting then and listening for boots *there they are no it's just the walls breathing there didn't you hear it no I didn't yes there it is again oh Jesus there's someone coming we're trapped how did they know betrayed I don't know someone's betrayed us what can we do like rats who's in there? stay still must stay still oh God oh God here they come*

Four o'clock

AND I wake suddenly to this: the sight of my new watch already rising luminous — and to thoughts, then, of other watches (here's that scattergun way leading on to way again) and other, distant close-up times. One time in particular, one watch — Fredzio's that had once been mine that had once been my father's that had once belonged to, well, no one will ever know now, will they? Which is not to say that it doesn't still exist under lock-and-key in some vault somewhere (the bomb having been, as it were, stillborn, its constituent parts quite lovingly though nervously deconstructed and its target, a tannery — no less, indeed, than Europe's, perhaps the world's, largest — left standing as it still stands today), and so, in theory at least, couldn't still be returned. In theory — although, of course, such a thing will never happen. All of *which*, ladies and gentlemen — this watch-stuff — I record here and now merely to illustrate the fact that — despite everything — despite what I believe to have been the last half an hour or so's unseemly ranting – I am still, at the very least, of sound sight and hearing (you should listen to this awful thing ticking: up close to your ear it's as loud and heavy-sounding as a grandfather clock), and that, consequently, my lawyer's assertion (you'll know Mr Sikorski by now, of course – he with the thick reading glasses and that tapping thing he does with the knuckles of his right hand on the back of his left) that, being as obviously crazy as I am, I can in no way be reasonably held responsible for my actions is not without its problems.

The most fundamental of which being, of course, that it's all just so much crap. Really – believe me – I know what I did: *I was there, don't forget, and I remember*. Yes, I remember that officer's face and, later, her face – I remember how sweetly familiar and comforting it was – and I remember how she sat there on her chair the other side of my desk, shifting herself this way and that as if she couldn't get comfortable, and how she pretended she didn't know that her skirt was riding up, and how all the time I was praying she'd stop it *and just leave me alone* – just let me get back to where I was on the page before everything came crashing in and something went click inside me and my head imploded –

But.

Right now, though, all of this is not so helpful, for, should these pages find their way to you, filled as they seem to be with such ludicrous melodrama, they would tend to give the lie to Mr Sikorski's defence – and don't misunderstand me, I do pray for acquittal every night – for the chance, then (my last, for sure), to make right those things I can make right. Such as Ewa, of course.

Ewa.

Oh of course I always knew in my heart that it would take

more than some wretched CD to bring her round. She is, after all, nearly nineteen – not fifteen. Which is something I know I should keep in my mind when dealing with her – that, and the fact that all this has been far from easy on her, what with the shame and the taunting she's been receiving (how *can* children be so cruel?) – not to mention her own severely compromised expectations.

So then.

The moment she returns – the moment I see her turning into Florianska Street – I shall prepare myself for the role in which lately I have been so deficient. Yes – you just wait and see. When that girl returns she's going to be seeing some changes. Oh yes. She's not going to know what's hit her.

First, though (and until then), it's Borowski, still, who does, I believe, deserve my attention. It is men like him, after all, who prove so costly to girls like my Ewa, and *should* be watched, by any and all who have the means.

Which, thanks to these binoculars (a pair of fine old things just this minute unearthed from the unlikely hiding-place of a box of children's toys), are means I have now in my possession.

So.

Here's looking at you, Borowski. Here's waiting and watching your every move.

Man with a mission

Well well.

Although I have long suspected him of being a man with another kind of secret too, I really had no idea until just now what it was. Well! And him always so nothing – so *ordinary*. Jesus. Sometimes people can *really* surprise you. Catch them unawares sometimes, when they think they can't be seen, and that's when they show you what lies within.

By which, of course, I don't just mean Borowski. I mean you too. And me. I mean everybody. I suppose it's just as well that all these terrible things stay mostly hidden, otherwise how could we live with one another, knowing that the woman next door – so staid, so dull during daylight hours – becomes a raging disco queen when night falls. Or that that couple you see every day in the park (oh how sweet they are, still holding hands after all these years!) are really plotting each other's death, he with a blade and she with the help of some ghastly – though entirely undetectable (of course) – poison.

No.

A life of reality would surely be unbearable.

Take Borowski, for example.

Or – better still, ladies and gentlemen – take me.

On the subject of which – that is, my own particular life of half-truths and deceit – a quite perfect irony occurs to me. It occurs to me (and only now for the first time – a curious thing, indeed, for someone so self-regarding) that for someone so keen on protecting the truth of things by underexposure to have in the end destroyed himself by (in the quaint and rather homely term) 'exposing himself' has about it a quite delicious symmetry. Indeed, were the likely consequences not so unpalatable (it seems I shall be 'exposed' again soon – this time publicly, for all to see), then it would be an act of balance of which I could be genuinely proud.

But.

Lest I continue down this track and say something my lawyer will regret, let me return to where I started on this.

Borowski.

Poor old Borowski.

Who on earth would have picked him for a fellow addict? Who would have put him sitting there, trousers around his ankles, his hand a blur before that flickering screen? Not I for one. Didn't think he had it in him.

Well.

Welcome to the club, Mr B!

Hurray! The Order of the Blurred Hand has another member.

But, yes, *seriously* now. I suppose I of all people should not be mocking the poor man and his unfortunate – what shall I say? Pastime? No – not me – particularly when, were it not for the unexpected chain of events that contrived to get me up here today, I would most probably be engaged in the same rather messy and ultimately depressing activity. (Of course I know my dear lawyer, Mr Sikorski, will be cutting this out, unhelpful as it is, no doubt, to his presumed presentation of me as someone quite 'normal', so what the hell . . .) Yes, I, too, would most probably be logged on and surfing the net (oh, how these terms fall so easily from my lips), pursuing through the ether those promises of *Cock-sucking cheerleaders* or girls (just eighteen, of course!) who'd like nothing more than to open their legs for me *and always with a smile.*

And smile they do – believe me. Look you directly in the eye, they do, as their fingers spread themselves; so direct, in fact, so straight at you, is their gaze always that, of course, one is forced, in no time at all, to look away, and then only sneak a look back when you're sure they must be bored or at least have moved on to someone else.

But of course they never have; they never do. Always they just sit there, their fingers gleaming and their eyes looking through you as if you're nothing (perceptive, these girls – cruel, but perceptive) and they're something special when all they really are are whores. Little more than children, some of them, but whores nevertheless. Oh, how they can bear to just sit there like that with snakes-in-the-grass like Borowski ogling them is beyond me. For heaven's sake, can they be so numb to embarrassment that even this . . . this . . . *exhibition* doesn't make them blush just a little? Surely, now and then, they must think of their mothers (not to mention their fathers) and wonder what *they'd* think if they knew?

I know what *I'd* think.

And I know what I'd *do*.

If it were *my* daughter out there – God forbid, if it were *Ewa* – then there's nothing I wouldn't do to rescue her from the gaze of men like Borowski. If necessary I'd hire someone to track her down – a private investigator or somebody – and then I'd sit her right down and teach her all I know about love –

About which you're an expert, of course.

Oh great. You're back.

Yes, I'm back. And you were saying –

I was *saying* how – step one – I'd sit her down and teach her about *love* and about *respect* for yourself and how, once they're gone, they're so difficult to get back, but that you can get them back if you really really try –

And step two?

Step *two* would have to do with Borowski and his kind –

His kind? And what's that exactly?

Oh, you know very well.

Oh I see.

See what?

What you're getting at.

I'm not getting at anything.

Yes you are. This is all just another roundabout way of saying what a terrible father I am –

Was. You're dead, don't forget.

How could I when you keep reminding me?

Oh why don't you just go back to sleep –

What? And miss step two?

What?

I mean, aren't you at least going to do something physical for once?

Oh, now it's my turn.

Your turn to what?

To see.

See what?

What you're getting at.

Well if the cap fits —

Fuck you.

No — fuck him.

What?

Borowski. Fuck Borowski. The traitor. It was him, *wasn't it?*

What?

You know what. Anyway, are you going to teach him a lesson or not?

All right, I will. If it'll shut you up.

Go on then. Tell us what you'd do. The ladies and gentlemen will be wanting some blood by now.

OK.

OK!

Now, ladies and gentlemen, I believe it's traditional in these kind of circumstances for the father to advocate the offender having his balls chopped off as if he was a dog or something. Well, that's all very well — but it's not what I'd do —

No sir? It isn't?

Oh no. Me? I'd chop off his arms at his elbows —

At his elbows? Now we're talking!

And why? Well, *that* way he'd still get a hard-on (assuming, of course, that he'd still be able to operate his computer somehow) —

A mere detail.

— but not be able to do anything about it. That would be the *real* killer. Yes, I'd sit here with these glasses just watching his agony as he stumbles around the room trying to find some relief. Now and then, of course, I'd fuck him up even more by calling up some whore and sending her round to his flat with instructions that whatever he says – however hard he begs her – she's never to touch him, but just to taunt him, until he's down on his knees and there's nothing he can do but watch her walk away and then listen as the door swings shut behind her. *Not,* you understand, that I'm at all a vindictive man –

No, no –

– I just know what is right and what is wrong. And believe me, Borowski and his kind are all wrong – and, I believe (though this is not popular I know), that they have been so wrong for so long now that they've become irredeemable and that no amount of saying you're sorry can possibly make any difference. They're rubbish, these people, and we need to face it. We need to accept the fact that half of humanity is worth nothing more than the shit on your shoes, and we need to accept it now – the sooner the better – before the evening comes on and the darkness falls and they step from the shadows and murder us all as we stand blind and fearful in the night.

And innocent. Blind, fearful and innocent, *don't forget.*

What?

What with the guilty having been – how shall we say? – liquidated.

Liquidated, yes. I like that.

You like that?

It's good.

Yes, it's good. Final, too. No coming back from it. No telling tales.

No more spreading lies.

I think we understand each other.

Because it's lying I can't stand.

Exactly. You know, I think we're on the same wavelength at last, you and me.

Oh, I don't know about that —

But then that's just as it should be, isn't it? I mean, after all, like father like son — isn't that what they say? Like father like son?

Dusk falls

AND again those fucking bells. And still those shadows lurching up and down against the wall.

God.

And there was I thinking the real thing was way out of his league.

I suppose it just goes to show how you never really get to know someone – never get to see what really makes up their lives – unless you catch them unawares. Only then – like now – will a person reveal himself.

But even so.

Borowski, for Christ's sake. With a real living whore. Now *that's* what I call hard to believe.

I suppose, being truthful, I have to admit that maybe I'm just a bit jealous. Not of the *sex*, you understand (believe me, I get all of *that* I want from my cyberwhores in cyberspace, with the added bonus, in their case, that they can neither talk back nor really look into my eyes) – no; it's more that I feel (and I know how weird this is going to sound) somewhat bereft. To tell the truth, having Borowski over there, jerking off in front of his screen while I was over here jerking off in front of mine, well, I'd begun to feel a certain wankers' camaraderie – like, tools in hand, we were pioneering some new kind of tossers' trade union, which one day – who knows? – could have blossomed into something really big. All of which glorious future, now, is gone of course. From now on, it seems, when I wank I wank alone.

But then, I suppose, I was a fool in the first place to believe in a man like Borowski – to believe such a man could be trusted to wank for the goodness of all, and not just for himself. I mean, after all, it's hardly the first time he's proved a disappointment.

Take, for example, all that talk about 'come the revolution' – how he'd be out on the street at the sound of the very first tank.

Well.

In fact, of course, he was nowhere to be seen; in *fact*, I found out later that, while me and Fredzio and Krysztof were making our own separate ways that day through the frozen streets, he – the Che Guevara of Florianska Street – was hiding heroically in the back of his mother's bedroom cupboard.

And to *think* –

Lord, to *think* –

Even now, after all this time, I can hardly bear to.

Lord.

How could we have been so blind? How could we not have seen the signs? All that bluster, all that range – all counterfeit: all just the fake cries for freedom of the coward secure in the knowledge of the hopelessness of his cause.

That – but maybe more.

Not, of course, that I can prove a thing. Proof of dissent disappears in defeat.

But I know.

I feel it.

After all, it was one of us.

And it wasn't Fredzio.

And it wasn't Krysztof.

Nor any of the other eleven.

No.

It was him.

Or me.

And it wasn't me of course.

So it had to be him. It had to be Borowski that broke the Rosary.

Yes.

And he'll pay.

Oh yes.

And with interest.

And soon.

Soon.

Four thirty

Now then.

I've been thinking.

Borowski.

When I said there was no evidence, what I meant to say was there was no evidence that would stand up in court. Not that courts ever really came into it – except, of course, the kind of courts that were rumoured to exist in the shadows well beyond the tarnished, yellow, sickly light of the law. Of these, of course, there was scarce (if any) evidence. Indeed, search for someone who'd freely admit to having attended such a court (or anyone who knew of another's attendance) and you could search for ever in vain.

Which is not to say that there wasn't the proof, plain for all to see.

Or not see.

The faces, for example, disfigured by the 'accidental' application of a burning cigarette; the family dogs found hanging by their leads in the stairwells of ten-storey blocks; the absences from work thanks to 'falls' on the Ryneck, and so on and so on.

Oh, and then there were the deaths, of course, the 'tragedies' in the home – those unfortunate 'accidents' caused by pans full of oil left casually unattended, or the unsecured carpets on busy flights of stairs.

All of which evidence, of course, was nothing of the sort. There were no investigations, and no charges were ever brought, for the heavy hand of the law had cast a depth of lawless shadow that only those of my father's generation could recognise. What goes around comes around, people say. Well, on that day and the days that were to follow, what had gone had for certain come back; what had once been to visit had now come to stay.

But, ladies and gentlemen, you would know all this – for, I assume, being a jury of my peers, you were there and you saw what I saw, and turned away, blind, from all that from which I turned away, also blind. Perhaps some of you were even neighbours of mine (this I won't remember, looking at you as I shortly will, as I've quite lost my memory for faces), or maybe we took the same courses at the university. Or maybe we were at school together (did I leave you out when choosing sides for football? Forgive me if I did, for I knew not what the stakes would become), or perhaps we went hiking together in the mountains.

Or perhaps – who amongst you now will say? – you were, back then, one of us – one of the band that wasn't going to stand for what, in the end, we so easily and so long stood for – one of the brotherhood whose brotherhood bled away in the endless snowy drifts, and whose will of iron would be crushed beneath another's will of steel.

Or perhaps –

But no.

Be careful what you say, my lawyer has advised me, *on no account antagonise*.

But fuck it.

And fuck *you*.

Maybe it was one of *you* and not our friend Borowski at all. Maybe it was *you*, sir, that betrayed us and forced us to scatter; maybe *you* were the one – or *you* – whose corruption brought Fredzio to his death in that schoolyard – *you*, who sit there now, in the comforting embrace of your armchair, enjoying the fruits of *his* labour.

Well, like I say – fuck you. Fuck you *all*.

But, then, you'll never get to read this anyway, will you? So why am I bothering? Why does anybody bother talking when they can't be heard? Why did so many offer prayers in the moment of their death? Didn't they know there was no one there to hear them? Or is that the point? Are we really praying to ourselves when we think we're praying to God?

But look at me. All this meandering has got me off-track. What, you'll be wondering, has happened to Borowski? And what of those shadows on the wall – how are they?

Well now.

Let me see.

At rest, I suppose you would say.

Yes, it seems like the man's run out of steam at last. Or money. Whatever, either way, the fun, for the moment at least, is, it seems, over.

Which leaves me, again, with nothing much to do but wait.

Wait for Ewa.

A situation which really, by now, should not surprise me at all. (In fact, I'm surprised that it does.) After all, sometimes it feels like I've done little else with my life except wait for Ewa. In the car in the street outside other children's parties; in the dark outside discos; with the telephone in my hand as she clomped her way down the stairs in those ridiculous shoes she used to wear. In fact, I've been waiting for Ewa ever since she was born — or rather, ever since that day at the hospital when she was *supposed* to be born, but for some reason refused to come out. For hours and hours I was waiting then, and then for days and days while Madam was deciding whether or not to make an appearance. Of course, that she finally *did* break out about two minutes after an emergency call from my tutor — a 'matter of life and death', or so he claimed (and with not a trace of irony) — had sent me out to the car park to once again try to start my old car, was, as it would turn out, just about typical. Not to mention the quite terrible distress her reluctant passage into life caused her mother, whose last words, as a consequence, were, I was thoughtfully informed, 'But where is my husband?'

Where is my husband?

Where indeed.

In the car park was where, studying the engine, quite hopelessly searching for something I wouldn't have recognised had I even found it. And all thanks to Ewa — or, perhaps, more fairly (and I must always strive to be fair), that call from my tutor, Professor (one day to be Dean) Nowak.

And the emergency? What was that? Was the building, after a thousand years' standing, crumbling suddenly and in such a way that only I could save it? Was an outbreak of cholera about to decimate the city whose only hope for an antidote lay with me? No to either of the above — oh no. The problem that had needed my so-urgent attention was far more earth-shattering than that.

Oh yes.

The life-and-death problem for which I abandoned my child-bearing wife – my beautiful Rachel – to a death amongst strangers was nothing less than a dog.

The *Nowak* dog.

The Nowak dog which, moments earlier, had been dis-covered hanging from its lead in the stairwell of their block. Yes, for this, and for the sake of two non-starting cars, I was absent when the only choice – mother or daughter – that ever mattered in my life was made.

And for this I should never be forgiven.

For this.

But not *just* for this.

For there is more.

There are others, beside me, who must pay. There are the masters of the universe with the gratuitous pornography of their inverted truth, and every pupil who ever sat, worshipful, at their knee. Yes, they must all pay as I have paid. And they *will* pay – of that make no mistake.

For the time is coming.

And soon.

But in the meantime?

In the meantime, I wait. I wait and I paste together my story. I seek forgiveness for what I've done by refusing to forgive those who did for me. I wait and wait – and then, every few minutes, I stand, in order to exorcise the stiffness from my limbs. And then, thus refreshed, I return to this window and wait some more.

And watch – don't forget watch.

What?

Borowski. You'll watch him, right?

I will.

Like a hawk?

Oh yes. I'll watch him like a hawk all right.

Like a hawk, in fact, with binoculars

OR, rather, like a hawk with binoculars who's been eating nothing but carrots for, say, the last twenty years.

What?

What do you mean, what?

I mean you're rambling again.

So I'm rambling. So what? Aren't you always telling me it's a free country?

Sure.

Well then.

I thought you said you had things to do. Your – what should I call them? – 'memoirs' to write. For that idiot Sikorski.

Oh for God's sake shut up.

Charming.

Just watch the street, will you?

Now your mother really would *be proud.*

Yes. About as proud of me as she was of you.

Fuck you.

I've just thought of a joke.

What?

A joke – I've just thought of a joke.

A joke?

Are you ready?

Jesus Christ almighty.

All right then. Here goes.

One day, while he's flying around and just minding his own business, Superman sees Wonderwoman spreadeagled on a rooftop. Now, as every schoolboy knows, the Man of Steel has always had a thing about Wonderwoman, so, seizing his opportunity, he swoops down and, without permission, has his wicked way. Anyway, when he's finished, he gets up and, while straightening his tights, says, 'And so what did you think of that?', to which the Invisible Man turns his head and says with a scowl, 'Well it didn't half hurt!'

I don't get it.

What do you mean, you don't get it? What's there not to get? It's the fucker fucked – right? One master of the universe taking it up the arse from another!

Jesus Christ.

And to think you people stand in judgement over *me*. Lord, is there no one out there who understands? Is there no one out there on my side?

Maybe my mother, my wife

Ah, son, let's not get confused.

I'm not confused.

With their high-polished boots –

What?

I said, with their high-polished boots and their strong and certain stride, when they walked they seemed to walk like the masters of the universe – like a race, it seemed, of barking supermen troubled neither by doubt nor hesitation –

Jesus Christ – what is all this?

A race, indeed, so convinced by their ice-god of the divinity of their purpose that it froze to subjugation all those at their mercy, those whose own exhausted God, though a loving God, had nothing, after so much fighting, left to offer – no means of useful combat but the mild insipid warmth of a slow-cooling corpse.

Hey –

'Raus!'

What?

'Raus! Raus!'

What the *fuck* are you saying?

And then, finally, with death's coming, the Lord Jehovah's once-great circus was silent, its overnight flitting leaving nothing in its place now but a hollow, pitted field. And men stared, no longer with the strength to be appalled, but just accepting now of such a soundless abandoning – of such a tepid withdrawal from the field. They looked to the sky and saw nothing there but grey; they looked to the future and saw nothing; they squinted at their palms, at the mocking laughter of their life-lines –

'Judemsweine!'

Then dumb, beaten low, they move slow along the road, shuffle out past the once-upon-a-time schoolhouse with its pale staring faces –

Twenty-one.

– Lumbering like cattle on their way to the slaughterhouse, there to be measured, graded, slaughtered.

Maybe today.

And skinned, some of them – the youngest and purest – while the others are discarded, kicked and heaved into pits.

Maybe today, he thinks. (He, that is I – was I.) Maybe today I'm a man. And look at me, he thinks. And he looks at his now-corrupted artist's hands, his arms, at his bundled-up, blood-frozen, black-and-blue feet. Today, he thinks, but then what is left of his mind, like the hard Polish earth, freezes over, and the thought remains for ever stillborn. He watches the others shuffle on, herding them as he himself is herded – the children and the men and the dried-up dying women – unaware, as they pass by the schoolhouse and the yard, of the squinting, loving eyes upon him.

Karolina, Karolina, wife-to-be.

And mother – don't forget mother.

Oh hear how, as she sees the young man (can it really be me?), her father's voice comes to her in memory, calling her in for her supper — for soup stiffly ladled from Aunt Joasia's china tureen, the one with the chip on the handle and the pattern of faded spring flowers.

At the window, now, her blunted fingers on the rotting sill, she feels again that chip in the china, sees again those faded flowers.

Karolina, Karolina. So long ago now.

She opens her mouth to answer her father — but nothing comes. There are too many years now between them, and far too many miles. Instead she just stares at the men, at the children as they pass.

At one man.

At me.

Papa?

Me, death's shepherd.

She thinks she whispers my name, but can't be sure. All she can be sure of is that she'll never see him again — that he'll never come back to her, that she'll never feel again the youthful desperation in his fingers as he touches her youthful ageing flesh — for she knows that she's not life enough left in her to care if he did. And besides, only they *come back, laughing like drunks in their bright, shiny boots, their cigarettes glowing like tiny fires in the dusk.*

And then always the Germans stop outside, as if nervous like schoolboys at a brothel, and always her heart and others' hearts shutter down and shrivel, try to hide, but in vain, in their thin, bony cages, as the boots crack the ice on their way across the yard, and stairs are mounted, and the terrible nightmare of night begins again.

Once, she remembers, as the last man is gone, once, in the ghetto, she'd found a piece of yellow cloth. It had been lying between her feet all the wretched hours of sleep, guarding her, she'd thought then, from all harm. Rising, bleary-eyed, she'd reached for it, gathered it as gently as you'd gather up a bird. She'd turned it over, turned it back. And she

feels she has it now; she raises it to her face, draws its scent into her
nostrils, feels in that instant — as if she'd really once felt it — the sudden,
fleeting warmth of his seed.

Karolina, Karolina.

Mama, Mama.

Standing, now, at that window, she feels herself sinking just that
little bit further (every new depth she reaches she feels surely must be her
last, her lowest) — not beneath the weight of her life's hope's extinguish-
ing (for that she has already mourned, and can mourn no more), but at
the loss, again (oh, how often she feels it, and how so acutely) of that
scrap of yellow cloth. She closes her eyes, tries to draw back the scent —
but cannot. It is gone, now, as surely as is the smell of her mother's
cabbage soup, and the feel of that tureen and its chip beneath her fingers
— as surely as the sound, on those long-gone afternoons, of her father
and his calling her to supper, then the crunching on gravel of his fine
leather shoes.

But for Christ's sake
that's all past, and

ANYWAY –

What?

Wake up.

What is it?

Something's happening.

You mean Borowski?

Who else? Look –

I can't see anything.

Use these.

OK.

Well?

I still can't see anything.

In the kitchen? You can't see what's happened? Are you saying you can't see?

That's what I'm saying.

Jesus Christ. Are you blind or what? Are you saying you can't see the knife?

The knife? Where?

And the blood – you're telling me you can't see the blood?

Blood? What are you saying?

I'm saying look, for God's sake –

Oh Jesus.

You got it?

I've got it.

Well, now do you believe me?

What the hell's been going on?

Two guesses.

What?

I said two guesses. I mean, just look at the place. Are you sure you need two guesses?

Oh God.

Now you've got it.

Oh God, oh God –

The man's been butchered.

Hah! The butcher butchered!

Tell me: what have you done?

What have I done? What do you mean, what have I done?

Jesus Christ –

Oh not Him again –

No –

What?

Wait a minute –

What do you mean, wait a minute?

I know what you're doing.

What I'm doing?

You're trying to fuck me up.

Fuck you up?

By lying.

About what?

Everything.

Everything?

You're just trying to make out it was me and not you –

Oh, it was me all right. Crept over there I did.

What?

You too, my boy. Are you saying you don't remember the ring of his bell?

No way.

Yes way.

No. You're just trying to fuck me up – trying to get me mad.

And why would I want to do that? You're my boy! I love you!

Oh, get out of here –

What?

Just get out, will you? Just get out and leave me alone.

So you can do what?

Things.

Things?

Yeah, things. I've got things to do.

Like what?

I've got a bicycle to fix.

A bicycle? Jesus, haven't you been listening at all?

And there's Mr Sikorski –

Oh Jesus. I didn't come here to fuck you up. And you know why? Because you're already fucked.

Just get out of here, will you?

Whatever you say, you stupid fuck.

Now. Right now.

OK. I'm going. But I'll be back. You can be sure of that.

Ah, just fuck off.

My pleasure. But don't forget what I said.

I'm not listening.

Yes we are.

I can't hear you any more I can't hear you any more I can't hear you any more I can't hear you –

Must think

MUST concentrate.

Banish all evil with the power of good.

So.

Think.

Happy thoughts – happy times, memories.

But *what* times, *what* memories? Have there *been* happy times? *Are* there happy memories?

Well, of course there are.

There's Rachel, for one. Our Austrian honeymoon. That week in Vienna. *I was thinking the Opera House then maybe some skiing.*

Oh yes. A happy memory indeed.

I remember especially the drive through Silesia to Cieszyn, how the March winds buffeted the car as if they were trying to turn it over, and how, once we'd crossed the border, the Czech police wouldn't leave us alone, and how (of course) we didn't care. All we cared about then was each other, and all the good things we knew the future had in store for us. Of course we didn't know then – then as, laughing, we pulled into Mikulov – that the future is a fickle thing and doesn't take kindly at all to predictions. But ignorance, more than ever, then, was bliss, and, that night, exchanging barbed wire for vines, both our ignorance and our bliss were complete – so much so, indeed, that that night in our bed at the Pension Schattner, we really believed that nothing, now, could touch us – that, with each other's warmth for protection, those winds, then, couldn't reach us, and that we were safe – then and in the future – safe, then, for ever and ever amen.

Safe?

Oh, such foolishness.

Safe.

Such fantasy.

Since when is a person in love ever safe? Since when was *that* particular border never more barbed wire than vine?

No.

A mistake, surely, this falling in love.

Yes.

A mistake.

And yet –

Oh for heaven's sake, what's wrong with me? Why can't I just let it – let *her* – be? Why can't I just leave it all behind me – let it all go as surely as is gone now that drive to the mountains – not to mention that hotel, that room, that bed? Why must I carry it all around with me still, as heavy and useless as stones in a backpack?

Well, the answer is I don't know.

Maybe it's just that that's the cost. Maybe happiness is a burden too – just like sadness – and just as heavy; and maybe, in the end, you've no choice but to shed it – to leave it on the roadside behind you – before its weight breaks your back, and, with it, any notions you once had of freshness, of renewal – any dreams you once harboured of living a clean, unencumbered life – a life not cowering stiffly before the threat of encirclement and then the slow starvation of a city besieged, and its gradual razing to ruins.

Ah, but listen to me: so little time, so much self-indulgence.

And to think I used to long for the quiet life of poets.

I must have been crazy.

But maybe you *have* to be crazy to make any sense of things.

But there I go again – off track.

So then.

Where was I?

Ah yes. The honeymoon. The hotel. The room. That bed.

How strange it is for me now – waiting, as I am, for the return of a fully grown woman – to think that it was in that small bed that she was made – to think that, after midnight (ten past the hour, to be precise; don't ask me how I know, I just know), there were suddenly the three of us, then, between those sheets and not just the two, and how crowded it suddenly was (although we didn't know it, of course – at least, not yet) and how crowded it would stay even after that day in the hospital – even until today – *until right now* – when, in truth, I couldn't be more alone.

So you believe me then – that she's not coming back?

Oh God, it's *you* again. I thought you'd gone.

Gone? But how could I go and leave you in such a state?

I'm not in a state.

I think you are.

OK, so maybe I'm just hungry. I mean, I haven't eaten since this morning. Since breakfast.

Oh, you mean since you and she had your little . . . chat.

What do you mean by that?

Oh, nothing.

No, come on. Tell me. I want to know.

No you don't.

Yes I do.

No you don't.

Oh Jesus – just tell me, will you?

You won't like it.

So I won't like it. So what?

OK. If you're sure . . .

I'm sure. Just get on with it.

Right. Well. You remember this morning – the talk you had with Ewa?

Of course I remember.

And you remember – do you? – how she said that friend of hers – what's his name –

Wojciech.

That's right.

Of course it's right.

Yes, of course. Well, anyway. You remember how she said he had some problem with his bicycle?

Of course I remember. I was there.

Well, the thing is . . .

The thing is what?

Well, he doesn't have a bicycle. Never did.

How did I know you were going to say that?

You did?

That you were going to say that, yes. That you were going to lie.

Lie? Why would I lie?

To try and keep us apart. You've always been jealous.

Jealous? You're crazy!

You've always hated her liking me more than you. Go on – admit it. You've always hated how she's always wanted me and wants nothing to do with you.

Is that right?

You know it is.

Then why did she scream?

What?

That last time. Why did she scream when you touched her?

That's a lie.

Is it? Why, then, if it's a lie, did she go and tell Dean Nowak?

She didn't. He just made it up.

Oh, so he's lying too.

Exactly. He's always hated me. He killed Rachel after all.

He did what?

You heard me. He called me away just when she needed me.

Called you away? You mean you had to go? You had no choice?

Exactly.

You mean he held a gun to your head?

Well no, of course not . . .

So you did have a choice: stay with your wife, or go and gloat over Nowak and his dog.

Well –

The dog that you hanged from a stairwell.

No, it wasn't like that –

No? Then how was it?

Oh, just leave me alone, will you –

Oh, very grown up. Very impressive. I'm sure Ewa really would have been proud –

Don't bring her into this.

She's in it.

I said –

Or was –

What?

I said she's in it already –

You said *was*.

Oh, so I did.

So, what do you mean? What have you *done*?

Done? Nothing. It was you that did something, don't forget.

Jesus Christ, you know something – don't you?

Know something? Like what?

I don't know.

OK.

OK?

I do know something.

I knew it –

I know how you sent me over there to teach that Borowski a lesson, and how he just wouldn't learn it, and so how, as a consequence, he had to be taught again, and again . . .

You mean? Oh God . . .

But he learnt it in the end OK, didn't he – finally knew the value of sacrifice? Didn't he squeal in the end and didn't we hear him say he was sorry? Oh, surely you remember that, don't you?

Oh God, oh God –

I mean, look at our shirt – here, smell it. Now, is that blood or is it blood?

What?

It's blood.

Jesus – what are you saying?

I'm saying, there's your evidence of a good job done. I'm saying it's over.

Over? What do you mean?

I'm saying a life for a life.

But –

But it wasn't Borowski? Is that what you're going to say? You think I don't know that? You think it matters? Oh no: it's the sacrifice that matters – blood for blood, and any blood will do.

No, you're crazy –

If I am, then so are you. And so are they to judge us. After all, they don't know what we know – haven't been where we've been.

But they know the truth –

The truth?

You *told* them –

Oh, you think they were listening?

Of course they were listening!

Then you really think they're there – out there. Jesus Christ, son – you really are in trouble.

But I heard them.

You heard no one.

But –

And no one knows. Just you and me. Son, the debt's paid. We're home free – don't you see?

No . . .

And I want to thank you, son.

Thank me?

For being so patient. You must know I'm so proud of you.

I don't understand.

Like father like son: no man could ask for more. So, again, thank you. And now I must leave you.

You're going?

Although there is just one thing.

What?

Your foot. Noticed anything?

Noticed what?

Never mind. Later. Right now I've things to do.

I don't believe a word of this.

It's the truth.

The truth?

Yes, the truth. You know what that is, don't you?

And the truth is

WELL, the truth is that all a man can do, if he cares at all for his soul, is, like Don Juan, agree to but a short armistice with the truth – for, in the end, the truth will not be denied, and will come back to haunt even the most robust of men, in the way that it has come back to haunt me.

Not, to be truthful now, that I am sorry for its haunting. In fact, I am glad of it. I am glad – grateful – for the chance that, by its coming, I am given to face that which has hitherto remained unfaced – turned away from – and to accept at last that which, up to now, has remained unaccepted.

This is just words.

Oh leave me be. Let me speak.

If you plan to.

I plan to. I am.

All right. But frankly I'm surprised.

Surprised?

That you can.

This is just one of your games.

What with your foot, I mean.

My foot?

I can't believe you haven't noticed.

Noticed? Noticed what?

I mean I've noticed – and it's not even my foot.

I don't know what you're talking about.

Oh come on. Can't you feel it now?

I can't feel anything.

Precisely.

Oh this is just more of your nonsense.

Feeling nothing's the point.

Oh, go away –

Tell me – is it the left or the right?

What do you mean?

That feels like nothing now.

Look, there's nothing wrong with my feet.

Try again.

Try what?

The left – try the left. Is it the left?

There's nothing wrong with it. Look –

Then it must be the right.

What?

Try it. Try moving it. I bet you can't, can you?

Of course I can.

Well go on then.

There.

You call that moving? Nothing happened. Do it again.

Oh God.

Him again!

What's going on?

What's going on? Life's what's going on, boy. My gift to you, if you like.

I can't feel it . . .

There, there –

It's gone to sleep –

Not to sleep, no.

It must have –

Look, just think about it, will you? Take some time. I promise you'll be glad.

Glad?

Just like me.

I don't understand –

You will, you will. And anyway, look on the bright side. Just think what it'll do to the jury – just think of the sympathy when they see they've got a cripple on their hands.

What?

But now I have to go.

Go?

Oh yes. I've work to do, don't forget. Other souls to, well, save.

But what about me? What about my foot?

Look, idiot, just because you can't feel it, it doesn't mean it's not there –

You mean it's not gone?

Of course not! Look – turn on that lamp if you don't believe me –

All right –

But not yet. Just give me a minute.

What's the matter now?

I can't explain. All I can say is you'll understand when it's your turn to pass that parcel.

My turn?

When it's you and Ewa –

And anyway, what lamp?

Goodbye then. For the moment at least.

Then you're coming back?

Yes. The schedule says once more. Anyway, as I said, goodbye.

Papa? Papa? Are you there, Papa? Can you hear me?

I *said*, the truth *is*

ALL right, all right
   You want the truth?
   You'll get the truth.
   The truth unvarnished, thus.
   But first —
   But no.
   Only joking.
   The time for all that's long past.
   Time now, ladies and gentlemen, as you say, for the truth.
   Which is.
   Well, the truth is that my father, dear man, never knew until
I told him — until I smothered him with the truth (with the
pressure of it — as surely as with the hand's force and pillow) —
quite how rich and twisted are the roots of our tree.
   The tree, that is, of life, ha ha.
   By which I mean.
   By which I mean he never knew until I told him — until I

hanged (or is it hung?) my head low before his as he lay there on his death-bed and whispered to him that which had once been whispered to me – those words of Rachel's which, then, made him, with his body's last breath, howl in his chains like a chained dog howls at midnight –

And they were – those words?

Ah patience, patience . . .

All right, all right.

At long last they were these.

My grandmother Karolina had a son – half Pole, half German – a camp-child conceived in what, ironically perhaps, had once, before the war, been a schoolhouse – and that son had a daughter –

A daughter?

A daughter. Me.

Me. That is – *her.* Rachel. Granddaughter of a German soldier and a Jew.

And that Jew was?

Well, my mother, of course.

And the German?

Franz Heppelmann, my father's – what? – foreman? Would that be right to say foreman?

Stop, please –

Oh, you're here too. Good. But anyway, as I was saying, he who died so bravely at the end of a Russian hangman's noose.

Janek, please –

There now.

That wasn't so hard, was it?

What do you mean – you people – you still don't see? What is it you don't see? That my mother and Rachel's grandmother were one and the same? Is *that* what you don't see?

Janek –

Or is there more?

Don't do it.

Can you not see the rest? Have you not guessed the extent of the horror?

It's gone. It's past. It's over.

But it's not over, Papa. It's never over. You saw to that, and made sure I pass it on –

I never.

Oh an end of lies, Papa. Let there be an end of lies.

Janek –

Let it end here, with us –

Enough, Janek, enough –

Not enough, no. Never enough. Now –

Oh, what now?

Now the truth, Papa, the whole truth –

I'll not hear it –

Well I'll not speak it – not to you, but to *them*. Now then, ladies and gentlemen –

Janek –

First, though, let us kill this rising gloom, lest the truth get lost once again in the shadows.

But how?

Oh, I know.

Bear with me, just bear with me –

But when you want,
of course, you can't find

AND it's only when you look you can't see. But then I
suppose a little darkness never hurt – and anyway, how could
I possibly think to find that old lamp now, here amongst all
this debris? Quite frankly, it could be anywhere – or, more
likely, nowhere. More likely, it's long gone – along, probably,
with all that other stuff the removal and destruction of which
so long ago now proved such an exercise in temporary
catharsis.

You know, it's a funny thing but, even now, sitting here, I
can feel again so strongly that sense of liberation I felt then, as,
standing amid those great heaps of ash at the municipal rubbish-
dump, I watched those great metal jaws bite down on and so
easily crush into nothing all that stuff from the past that had
seemed for so long indestructible – and how I'd really thought
the relief would last. But no – I should have known better. I
should have known that, in the end, it is only through facing
things and saying their names out loud that the least and the

most amongst us can find his rest – and that only then can those who've wandered so far from God's stifling embrace find peace and an end to their wandering.

Speaking of which

DID I mention how somebody – a Jew – once told me that in Israel it's illegal to use a mobile phone in any public place? No? Well, apparently (according to Moshe, our dedicated visiting professor of rhetoric), anyone caught so doing will be deemed to have been taking part in (I think he said) '*clandestine activities contrary to the security of the state*', and could therefore be liable to face a charge of treason or terrorism (or something), although, according to Moshe, a charge of disturbing the peace would be more likely, followed by a pretty hefty fine.

And all because people get pissed off at the noise.

Wonderful.

Talk about people power.

Here, of course, everyone could go around using bloody megaphones and nothing would get done. If they did, and you complained, most likely you'd get your windows mysteriously broken at night, or some dog-shit that really stains the carpet and sticks to your shoes pushed through your letterbox. And if you dared to complain about that – well, you would, of course, be accused of being an anti-Semite, which, in my case at least, would be ridiculous. I mean, after all, what could possibly be better and more convincing evidence of a person's tolerance for the beliefs of another race than for that person to marry (and, what's more, have a child with) a *member* of that race?

But oh no. Is that enough?

It is not.

It is not – would not be – enough for me – just as it was never enough for my father.

You know, sometimes I think I can never do enough – all of which, sometimes, makes me think why should I bother doing anything? Sometimes, it even makes me think, well, as I've already been accused, tried and found guilty, and, consequently, I'm already serving some kind of a sentence, then why not go out and have a bit of fun with the crime? I mean, what more could they do to me that they've not already done?

Watching, waiting

WATCH with me now the darkness falling on the street. Hear with me the sounds of the dying day. Borowski's flat is silent now, his rooms all stillness and shadows. And down in the street, people hurry on home, anxious to beat the night's curfew. A dog – not seen, but heard. A sudden inexplicable whistling – then nothing. Just the arms of the night enfolding, muffling, choking.

I remember those glassless rooms, the draughts beneath those old schoolhouse doors.

Come huddle with me now, bunched up – out of reach (for the moment at least) of the moon's acid fingers.

And I remember, on cold mornings, breaking ice on the surface of puddles in the yard, and the sharpness like claws of the water trapped beneath.

And listen with me now to the ringing of a telephone.

And, in summer, how the ground was harder than teeth, harder even than bone.

Listen.

There.

Hear with me now how, finding no one at home, the ringing shrugs its shoulders and walks away.

Before the glass in the windows was shattered for sport, and boots filled the yard —

Oh listen to that silence now approaching.

And Germans filled the boots and took all the air.

Hear the scraping of its jewel-encrusted scabbard on the stairs. Hear how grudging is its breath — how unwilling its filth-corrupted lungs.

Shenandoah.

Oh Papa —

You know I'd seen her first — your mother — behind the bars of a glassless window, just as the light was dimming and night coming on, the gentle slope of her young girl's shoulders — saw how she looked so tiny, like maybe she would fit in my pocket.

Don't you know you have come so far, and yet no distance at all?

I know it.

Oh Papa, Papa — wretched widower, too, of the schoolhouse — why did you come back at all? Don't you know that your girl — your wife — is no longer here — hasn't walked these streets now for nearly thirty years? Don't you know that the earth, still so hard in summer and harder still in winter, will not — *cannot* — give her up? Don't you know that it has consumed her bones now — just as the lime, long ago, scorched and swallowed the flesh of so many?

Go home, Papa, go home —

I am home, I am —

Don't stand any longer in the ruins of that house, scouring

the rubble for those pale slender hands. Don't search the darkness any more for the slope of those shoulders. And don't look at me that way when we pass in the corridor, or sit together, talking, on the tram. And, above all, don't forgive my tainted blood, nor the shallow heart that pumps it. No: curse me on cold mornings as I have cursed you.

I do, I do –

I cannot stand any longer the touch of your hand clasped in greeting.

Oh Papa, Papa.

In my heart I wish you were dead too.

But you are not dead.

I am with you –

You are with me now, *there* (I can see you), standing in the shadows outside the Mleczko Gallery, your face so pale, the tip of your shoe caught sharp as a diamond in the moon's piercing stare.

Turn away, turn away.

I cannot –

Then why must you stare so?

For when I turn, you turn too.

What is it you are hoping to find?

We turn together now.

Believe me, whatever it is – whether guilt, remorse, whether hatred – you will not find it here. Not any longer. All you will find now – all anyone will find when eventually they come for me – is a shallow empty space, enclosed by the cold bone and flesh of a stiffening corpse.

Don't tell me what I already know – tell them.

Which brings me, dear friends – dear gentlemen and ladies of the jury – to my plans for the future.

Tell them how we're tired, so tired now –

I wish (of course) for my body to be burnt.

Tell them how the cursed curse and cannot stop –

And flowers.

None.

Except through blood and an end of blood –

And speeches.

None.

Except through God's blessing of childlessness – of fingerprints wiped clean and of earth scorched and burned –

Just the sound, if you can manage it, of a hundred keys in a hundred locks, and the hits of Frankie Valli and the Four Seasons playing low on the stereo.

Oh tell them –

'Oh What a Night' especially.

Tell them we are one now –

And others of course.

One source – isolated, concentrated for ease of destruction.

'Rhapsody', for one.

Tell them now, while there's time –

No.

No?

'Silver Star' for another.

But you must – how else will it ever end?

And 'Rag Doll', and 'Big Girls Don't Cry' –

Janek –

You tell them.

What?

I said, you tell them. I am not you. You are not me. The history is yours – not mine. We are not one.

But, Janek, history bleeds. It runs like a river. I run into you as you run into Ewa. Oh it runs like a river –

Then damnit.

I cannot.

It was a joke.

A joke?

I am not listening.

But Janek —

Not listening not listening —

Janek!

Not listening not listening not listening not listening not listening not listening not listening not listening not listening not listening not listening not listening not listening not listening not listening not listening not listening

Learn how to say goodbye

You really have to hand it to Paul Anka. Surely only a man of his genius could write a song in which explicit reference is made to the act of abortion, without the whole thing getting too unpleasant for words. But this is exactly what he achieves with the entirely masterful '(You're) Having My Baby'. '*Didn't have to keep it,*' he sings, '*wouldn't put you through it*' – and all in that wonderfully evocative voice of his – the voice of a man who, for sure, you just know really has faced these (and other) terrible dilemmas.

Oh yes.

Paul Anka.

Nobody can touch him for hitting right at the heart with the questions of the day.

Oh I really could go on . . .

But I won't – not now. Now, instead (although it hurts me to leave Mr Anka aside), I shall address myself to the question which I know, ladies and gentlemen of the jury, has been exercising the not inconsiderable powers both of your individual and collective minds – namely, that is, just exactly what *did* happen at that schoolhouse, and why, for heaven's sake, did Frankie Valli and the Seasons never once come to Poland? I mean (on this second question) it's not as if we don't buy records here – and, besides, what other nation could boast a Socialist Youth for the Four Seasons Appreciation Party, complete with quarterly hand-printed magazine?

Oh, you don't believe me?

Well take a look at this – and see (if your eyesight permits you – mine, sadly, now does not, although short-sightedness, sometimes, is rather less than a curse) just who it is that held the offices both of Chairman of the Party *and* Events Co-ordinator?

Janek?

Yes, of course!

Do you see what I see?

What?

Oh Lord, there she is, Janek, there she is –

What do you *mean* you don't believe a word of it? What do you mean oh God oh God oh God *oh God oh God oh God her face at that glassless window is she watching me or is she long past seeing anything but a past long gone I don't know I don't care the children walk on hobbling on their tiny bandaged feet lucky to get them but there's always a price for everything isn't there but you wouldn't understand that what choice did I have and if you had the same choice wouldn't you do the same or worse and believe me there is worse much worse like what they do can't stop them so what's the point the whole world is shit now so what does it matter what does anything matter oh Jesus oh Jesus what have I done am I doing oh what in the name of God would the man I was a man once say if he could only see what I am now what they've made me but no no no not think like that not think at all thinking is gone now the time for it all I can do is look see if she's watching but slyly under my arm like this Hey you what the fuck are you doing keep in line you step out one more time you even look at me you piece of shit and you're fucking dead do you understand I said do you understand Jesus Christ these fucking Yids they still think they're gonna live even when they hear that shooting even when they see the pits and that smell that comes over you and makes your eyes stream it's the lime it can burn you if you're not careful and even if you are I mean just look at these hands they used to be so beautiful tanner's hands you've got the hands of an artist everyone used to say but not now now they're all callouses and sores and I fucking told you I fucking told you didn't I fucking tell you are you fucking deaf or something here take this you piece of shit oh no not you darling you come with me oh so smooth so smooth really work with that just one more what does it matter what does anything matter I wouldn't mind but maybe after the war Karolina you and me could go out sometime do you think so four then shall we make it four shall we meet on the Ryneck beneath the clock I know a nice place hey you yes I said you what do you think you're looking at you think I give a shit what you think get up get up get up all right stay there see if I care you're all dead anyway what's that oh no don't you know he's not coming don't you know that god of yours doesn't care about you any more say goodbye say goodbye yes it's really nice maybe we could go and take a walk by the river oh it's so beautiful don't you think at this hour do you think I could kiss you oh please let me kiss you don't you know I'm starving inside too and I'm so so cold*

Yellow skin, yellow cloth

ONLY now, by lamplight, do the numbers appear. They were blurred at first, but are growing sharper now, each one a slightly different depth of black, though each with a bluish hue, and all set with a quite exhilarating neatness within my wrist's jaundiced-looking flesh – flesh cast so by the shade's yellowed membrane.

Skin.

Skin.

A tiny scrap of cloth.

Oh how necessary is skin for this wonderful and ludicrous business of living – and how, in the end, as with all things handed down, inescapable. Oh I should have known this – me of all people. I should have known, for example, and long ago, that it is only through the loving benevolence of a sharpened tanner's blade that the belly of the beast may be split in two and the soul trapped within find release, and that only through the flow of such blood as this as this as this as this that the hands of the father, the son and the unholy spirit may at long last be washed and made once and for evermore clean.

A NOTE ON THE TYPE

The text of this book is set in Linotype Sabon, named after
the type founder, Jacques Sabon. It was designed by
Jan Tschichold and jointly developed by Linotype,
Monotype and Stempel,in response to a need for a typeface
to be available in identical form for mechanical hot
metal composition and hand composition using
foundry type.

Tschichold based his design for Sabon roman on a fount
engraved by Garamond, and Sabon italic on a fount
by Granjon. was first used in 1966 and has proved an
enduring modern classic.